# ROYAL COURT

Royal Court Theatre presents

# HARVEST
by **Richard Bean**

First performance at The Royal Court Jerwood Theatre Downstairs
Sloane Square, London on 2 September 2005.

# HARVEST

by **Richard Bean**

Cast
Mam/WAC Officer **Sharon Bower**
Laura **Siân Brooke**
Warcliffe/Lewis **Mike Burnside**
William **Matthew Dunster**
Albert/Alan **Gareth Farr**
Danny **Craig Gazey**
Maudie **Jane Hazlegrove**
Titch **Adrian Hood**
Vet **Clare Lams**
Parker/Blue **Paul Popplewell**
Stefan **Jochum Ten Haaf**
Lord Primrose Agar/Young Agar **Dickon Tyrrell**

Director **Wilson Milam**
Designer **Dick Bird**
Lighting Designer **Paul Keogan**
Sound Designer **Gareth Fry**
Assistant Director **Elina Männi**
Casting **Amy Ball, Lisa Makin**
Production Manager **Paul Handley**
Stage Manager **Maxine Foo**
Deputy Stage Manager **Claire Casburn**
Assistant Stage Manager **Nafeesah Butt**
Stage Management Work Placement **David Somers**
Costume Supervisor **Jemimah Tomlinson**
Wigs and Make-up **Pam Humpage**
Fight Director **Bret Yount**
Company Voice Work **Patsy Rodenburg**
Dialect Coach **Neil Swain**
Set Builder **Scott Fleary Ltd**

# THE COMPANY

**Richard Bean** (writer)
For the Royal Court: Honeymoon Suite (English Touring Theatre); Under the Whaleback, Toast (co-production with RNT Studio).
Other theatre includes: Mr England (Sheffield Crucible/RNT Studio); The Mentalists (RNT); Smack Family Robinson (Newcastle Live!); The God Botherers (Bush).
Opera includes: libretto for Paradise of Fools (Unicorn Arts Theatre).
Radio includes: Of Rats and Men, Control Group Six, Unsinkable, Robin Hood's Revenge.

**Dick Bird** (designer)
For the Royal Court: Flesh Wound.
Other theatre includes: Lear (Crucible); The Night Season, A Prayer for Owen Meany and The Walls (RNT); Tejas Verdes, Marathon (Gate); By the Bog of Cats (Theater Heilbronn); The Wind in the Willows, The Lady in the Van (West Yorkshire Playhouse); Dirty Wonderland, Rabbit, Heavenly, Peepshow (Frantic Assembly); The Three Musketeers, Monkey! (Young Vic); Defence of the Realm (Peacock Theatre, Dublin); La Boheme (English Touring Opera); Mr Placebo (Traverse); Great Expectations, True West (Bristol Old Vic); The Banquet (Protein Dance); Thwaithe (Almeida Opera); La Cenerentola (Opera Theatre Company, Dublin); Die Kunst Des Hungerns (Schauspielhaus, Graz); The Lucky Ones (Hampstead); Messalina (Battignano Opera Festival); Ben-Hur (BAC); The Invisible College (Salzburg Festival); Vollo Di Notte and Il Tabarro (Long Beach Opera Company, California); Light (Theatre de Complicité); Closer, My Fair Lady (Teatro Broadway, Buenos Aires); Icarus Falling, Poseidon, Vagabondage (Primitive Science).

**Sharon Bower**
For the Royal Court: How Now Green Cow.
Other theatre includes: A Patriot for Me (Leeds Playhouse); Like Dolls or Angels (Royal Exchange, Manchester); Romeo and Juliet (Young Vic); The Daughter-in-Law (Crucible, Sheffield); Princess Ivona (Lyric, Hammersmith); Thark, Romeo and Juliet, She Stoops to Conquer, Jumpers (York Theatre Royal); Nicholas Nickleby (RSC/Aldwych/New York); Baal, Pericles, The Accrington Pals (RSC/Donmar).
Television includes: Casualty, Touching Evil, Traffik, Oranges are not the Only Fruit, The Bill, Landing on the Sun, Nicholas Nickleby.
Film includes: Among Giants, Tom and Viv, The Bounty, Bridget Jones's Diary.

**Siân Brooke**
For the Royal Court: Just a Bloke, The One with the Oven.
Other theatre includes: The Greater Good Absolutely Perhaps (Wyndham's); Romeo and Juliet, King Lear, Poor Beck (RSC).
Television includes: All About George, Under the Greenwood Tree, Dynotopia.
Radio includes: Murder on the Home Front, Dreaming in Africa (Radio 4).
Sian graduated from RADA in 2002.

**Mike Burnside**
Theatre includes: Christmas Carol, Twelfth Night, Spring Awakening, A Midsummer Night's Dream, The Venetian Twins, The Tempest, Love's Labour's Lost, King Baby, The Glowing Manikin, Christie in Love (RSC); The Seagull, Taking Steps, Mrs Warren's Profession, Candlelight (tour); When the Wind Blows (Southwark); Charley's Aunt, The Real Inspector Hound, Twelfth Night, Funny Peculiar, The Lady's Not for Burning, Ten Little Indians, Toad of Toad Hall, Bent, School for Scandal, Lloyd George/My Father, Show Boat, Two Planks and a Passion, Perchance to Dream, You Never Can Tell, Treasure Island, The Deep Blue Sea, Absurd Person Singular, The Recruiting Officer, Rosencrantz and Guildenstern are Dead, Hamlet, Othello, Aladdin, Flare Path, Love's Labour's Lost, The Dresser, Dandy Dick, Murderer, Dear Brutus (Northcott); How the Other Half Loves (Palace, Watford); Tropical Tree (Hammersmith, Lyric); King Lear (Bristol Old Vic); The Recruiting Officer (Chichester Festival Theatre); The Beggar's Opera (Wilton's Music Hall); Tropical Tree (Edinburgh); In Love with Anton (King's Head); An Empty Plate in the Café du Grand Boeuf (New End); The Madness of King George III (RNT); Volpone (Almeida); To Kill a Mockingbird (Mermaid); Funny Peculiar (Northbank); Camille, Pravda, All's Well that Ends Well (Leeds); Svejk, The Adding Machine, Leonce and Lena, Hitler in Liverpool, One Orange for the Baby, Up in the Hide, Gringo Planet (Gate).
Recent television includes: The Alan Clark Diaries, The House That Jack Built, American Embassy, Pure Wickedness, Family Affairs, The Bill, Noble and Silver, Vanity Fair, Mosely, Eastenders, Cats Eyes, Bergerac, Enemy at the Door.
Recent film includes: Charlotte Gray, Silent Cry, Virgin, Welcome to Ibiza, Criminals, The Pardoner's Tale, The Plague, Perfect Day, The Housewife.
Recent radio includes: Daughters of Britannia.

**Matthew Dunster**

For the Royal Court: Under the Whaleback, Plasticine, Toast.

Other theatre includes: Permanent Way (RNT/Out of Joint); The Daughter-in-Law (Young Vic); The Outsider, The Trial, The Mill on the Floss, Cinderella: the Play (Contact); But the Living are Wrong in the Sharp Distinctions They Make, Nest of Spices (Newcastle Playhouse); Happy Families (Derby Playhouse); Road (Royal Exchange); Fallen Angels (Fecund Theatre); Project C: On Principle (The Work).

Television includes: Heartbeat, Murder Prevention, Blue Blood, No Angels, Doctors, Coronation Street, Gimme Gimme Gimme, Casualty, Always and Everyone, Spring Hill, Brookside, New Voices, Golden Collar, Into the Fire, Conviction Murder Prevention.

Film includes: Hello You, Peaches.

Writing includes: Tell Me (Contact); Two Clouds Over Eden (Manchester Royal Exchange).

Directing includes: Project B (The Work); Some Voices (Young Vic); Port Authority (Liverpool Everyman).

Matthew is an Associate Director of the Young Vic and a founder member of The Work Theatre Collective.

**Gareth Farr**

Theatre includes: Fen, Sharp Relief and Taming of the Shrew (Salisbury Playhouse); A Midsummer Night's Dream (RSC/international tour); Parting Shots (Stephen Joseph Theatre); Hobson's Choice (Young Vic/tour); Brassed Off (York Theatre Royal); Romeo and Juliet (Derby Playhouse).

Television includes: Heartbeat, The Bill, Turkish Delight, Jonathon Creek, A Life Beyond The Box, Sin.

**Gareth Fry** (sound designer)

Gareth trained at the Central School of Speech & Drama in theatre design. His work as a sound designer and occasionally as a composer includes: For the Royal Court: Talking to Terrorists (with Out of Joint); Forty Winks, Under the Whaleback, Nightsongs, Face to the Wall, Genoa 01(with Complicite); Redundant, Mountain Language, Ashes to Ashes, The Country, Holy Mothers.

Other theatre includes: Theatre of Blood, Fix Up, Iphigenia at Aulis, Three Sisters, Ivanov, The Oresteia (RNT); Strange Poetry, Noise of Time, Mnemonic (Complicite); Macbeth (Out of Joint); World Music, The Dark (Donmar); Astronaut (Theatre O); Chimps (Liverpool Playhouse); Giselle (Fabulous Beast); By the Bog of Cats (Wyndham's); Blithe Spirit (Savoy); Zero Degrees and Drifting (Unlimited); Time & Space (Living Dance Studio, Beijing); Shape of Metal (Abbey, Dublin); Living Costs (DV8 at Tate Modern); The Watery Part of the World (BAC); A Midsummer Night's Dream (Regent's Park); Eccentricities of a Nightingale (Gate, Dublin); Mr. Placebo (Traverse); Forbidden Broadway (Albery); Accrington Pals (Chichester); Wexford Trilogy (OSC); Play to Win (Yellow Earth).

**Craig Gazey**

Theatre includes: 'Tis Pity She's a Whore (RWCMD/Bristol Old Vic); Poor Cousin (RWCMD/Hampstead); I Licked a Slag's Deodorant (Venue 13/RWCMD), Uncle Vanya, The Pitchfork Disney, As You Like It, The Country Wife, Guys and Dolls (RWCMD).

Television includes: Caerdydd, 3/7/11.

Radio includes: The Laramie Project.

Craig recently graduated from the Royal Welsh College of Music and Drama.

**Jane Hazlegrove**

For the Royal Court: Herons.

Other theatre includes: Sing Yer Heart Out for the Lads (RNT); Mammals, Wishbones, Boom Bang-a-Bang, The Mortal Ash (Bush); The Accrington Pals (West Yorkshire Playhouse); The Wolves (Paines Plough tour); Heartbreak House (Coventry); My Mother Said I Never Should, Blood Wedding, Billy Liar, Time and the Conways, An Inspector Calls, The Importance of Being Earnest, All in Good Time, (Bolton); The Crucible (Manchester Library); To Kill a Mockingbird (Contact).

Television includes: Buried (BAFTA for Best Drama), Silent Witness, Without Motive, The Cops, Hero to Zero, London's Burning, Making Out, The Bill, Faith, Judge John Deed, Heartbeat, Dalziel and Pascoe, Inspector Lynley Mysteries, Holby, You Can't Be Too Careful, The Grand, Jonathan Creek, Band of Gold, Shooting Star, Lovejoy, A Touch of Frost.

Film includes: Cheeky, Heidi, The Whipping Boy, About Time, Herbert's Balls.

**Adrian Hood**

Theatre includes: Fly me to the Moon, Our House (Hull Truck); Perfect Pitch, Salt of the Earth (Hull Truck/national tour); Up'n' Under (Liverpool Playhouse/West End); Up'n' Under II (UK national tour); The Rise and Fall of Little Voice (RNT/Aldwych); Stirrings in Sheffield (Crucible); Salt of the Earth (Octagon); Bouncers (national tour); The Jungle Book (Cumbernauld); Weekend Breaks (West Yorkshire Playhouse).

Television includes: Oddsquad, The Royal, Sweet Medicine, Thunder Road, Buried, Stan the Man, Heartbeat, The Bill, Victoria Wood with all the Trimmings, Micawber, Where the Heart is, Dinner Ladies, All Quiet on the Preston Front, Witness Against Hitler, Harry, Stay Lucky, My Kingdom for a Horse, Small Zones.

Film includes: Brassed Off, Up'n' Under.

**Paul Keogan** (lighting designer)
Theatre & opera includes; Blue/Orange (Sheffield Crucible/UK tour); Born Bad, In Arabia We'd All Be Kings (Hampstead); Too Late for Logic (Edinburgh Festival); Shimmer, Olga (Traverse); The Silver Tassie (Almeida); The Tempest (Theatre Royal Plymouth/UK tour); The Makropulos Case, Un Ballo in Maschera, Der Fliegende Holländer (Opera Zuid, Netherlands); The Queen of Spades, Madama Butterfly, Lady Macbeth of Mtensk, The Silver Tassie, (Opera Ireland); The Lighthouse (Opera Theatre Company); The Electrocution of Children, Amazing Grace, Living Quarters, Making History, The Map Maker's Sorrow, Cúirt an Mheán Oíche, Mrs Warren's Profession, Bailegangáire, Eden, The Wild Duck, The Cherry Orchard, Defender of the Faith, Portia Coughlan, Heavenly Bodies (Abbey/Peacock); Chair, Angel Babel, Here Lies (Operating Theatre); La Musica, Shutter (Siren Productions); Trad (Galway Arts Festival); The Sugar Wife (Rough Magic); Family Stories and Tejas Verdes (B*spoke). Future projects include The Wexford Opera Festival and Titus Andronicus (Siren Productions).

**Clare Lams**
Theatre includes: Chimps (Liverpool Playhouse); Soap, Fields of Gold (Stephen Joseph); Citizenship, Portrait of a Girl in Glass (RNT); Huddersfield, Coming Around Again (West Yorkshire Playhouse); The Happiest Days of Your Life (Royal Exchange); The Dice House (Birmingham Stage Co); Romeo and Juliet (Shakespeare in the Park).
Television includes: The Brief, The Bill, Eastenders.
Film includes: Southwalk the Movie, Cerberus, Sputnik Sweetheart, Crosspin.

**Elina Männi** (assistant director)
As a director theatre includes: Our Little Destabilisation (Camden People's Theatre); Vagina Monologues (Ugala Repertory Theatre, Estonia); Machinal (White Bear); Dossier: Ronald Akkerman (Finborough); Funny House of a Negro, Gone Out (Rose Bruford); Mouthful of Birds (SFA Downstage Theater, USA); Streetwise (Union); Euston Language (King's Head); Rainbow Conversation (Arcola).
Elina is currently trainee director on attachment at Royal Court, with support of the Channel 4 Theatre Directors' Scheme Bursary (sponsored by the Harold Hyam Wingate Foundation).

**Wilson Milam** (director)
For the Royal Court: Fresh Kills, Flesh Wound (& Galway Arts Festival).
Theatre includes (UK and Ireland): Chimps (Liverpool Playhouse); Defender of the Faith (Abbey, Dublin); True West (Bristol Old Vic); Mr. Placebo (Traverse); Lieutenant of Inishmore (RSC Stratford/Barbican/Garrick/tour); On Such As We (Abbey, Dublin); A Lie of the Mind (Donmar); The Wexford Trilogy (Tricycle/Lowry/Gateway); Hurlyburly (Old Vic/Queen's); Bug (Gate, London); Killer Joe (Traverse/Bush/Vaudeville).
US theatre includes: Closer (Berkeley Rep); Bug (Woolly Mammoth, Washington DC); Killer Joe (Soho Playhouse/29th St. Rep, New York/Next Theater, Chicago); Pot Mom (Steppenwolf, Chicago); Caine Mutiny Court-Martial (A Red Orchid, Chicago); Skeleton (Shattered Globe, Chicago).
Radio includes: Dr. Who-Scream of the Shalka.

**Paul Popplewell**
Theatre includes: The Shy Gas Man (Southwark); Under the Whaleback, A Christmas Carol (Sheffield Crucible); The Modernists (Hull Truck); American Buffalo (Royal Exchange); Bad Weather, The Tempest, Bartholomew Fair (RSC); Torch Song Trilogy, Romeo and Juliet, Love Kevin, Bugsy Malone (Northern Theatre Co).
Television includes: The Somme, Ghost Squad, Totally Frank, Caravaggio, The Royal, Gifted, Casualty, Rehab, Alan Partridge, The Bill, Doctors, The League of Gentlemen, Peak Practice, Heartbeat, Hetty Wainthrop Investigates, The Wedge, Island, Out of the Blue, Criminal, Kid's Court.
Film includes: Bright Young Things, 24hr Party People, Morvern Callar, In This World, Club le Monde, I Want You, If Only (Twice upon a Yesterday), Fairytale: A True Story.
Radio includes: Trapped, Visiting Time, Plasticine, Bad Weather.
Awards include: Golden Chest International Film and TV Festival Best Actor. Nominated for Best Actor at the Royal Television Awards. Nominated for Best Supporting Actor at the Manchester Evening News Awards.

## Jochum Ten Haaf

Theatre includes: Mourning Becomes Electra (Theatre Group, Amsterdam); Vincent in Brixton (ATG/Golden Theatre/Lincoln Center/Wyndham's/ RNT); The Importance of Being Earnest (National Theatre, Holland); 'T Zal Je Kind Maar Wezen Revisited, Arturo Ui, Othello, Who's Afraid of Virginia Woolf?, True Romance, U.S. Amok (Noord Nederlands Toneel TC); Knights of the Round Table (Blue Moon Festival).
Television includes: Spangen, Bad Girls, Medea.
Film includes: Tulse Luper, Code 46, De Erfenis, Pulp, The Athlete of the Century, Amazones: Yu-Lan and Lisa.

## Dickon Tyrrell

Theatre includes: The Merchant of Venice (Japan, China, Malaysia, USA), Henry IV, Richard II, Richard III, The Devil is an Ass, Julius Caesar (RSC); Major Barbara (Peter Hall Company); Misanthrope (Piccadilly); Romeo and Juliet, Antony and Cleopatra, The Passion, The Blood of Dracula, A Midsummer Night's Dream (Northern Broadsides); Romeo and Juliet (Contact); Ninagawa's Peer Gynt (international tour); Much Ado about Nothing (West End); The Taming of the Shrew, The Plough and the Stars (West Yorkshire Playhouse); Seven Doors (Gate); Coriolanus, Blood Wedding (NYT).
Television includes: Doctors, Peak Practice, Harry, Spender, The Beautiful South (Dream a Little Dream).
Radio includes: Antony and Cleopatra, Major Barbara.
Directing includes: Shakespeare in the Square (NYT).

## ACKNOWLEDGEMENTS

The Royal Court would like to thank the following for their help with this production: Bicycle Workshop, BlackBerry, City Mobility, English Touring Theatre, Independent Living Company, Frantic Assembly, Hampstead Theatre, Keep Able, Kellogg's, Geraldine Rushden, Shared Experience Theatre, Rose Bruford College, Rotech, Stone Crabs, Tate & Lyle.

## THE ENGLISH STAGE COMPANY AT THE ROYAL COURT

The English Stage Company at the Royal Court opened in 1956 as a subsidised theatre producing new British plays, international plays and some classical revivals.

The first artistic director George Devine aimed to create a writers' theatre, 'a place where the dramatist is acknowledged as the fundamental creative force in the theatre and where the play is more important than the actors, the director, the designer'. The urgent need was to find a contemporary style in which the play, the acting, direction and design are all combined. He believed that 'the battle will be a long one to continue to create the right conditions for writers to work in'.

photo: Andy Chopping

Devine aimed to discover 'hard-hitting, uncompromising writers whose plays are stimulating, provocative and exciting'. The Royal Court production of John Osborne's Look Back in Anger in May 1956 is now seen as the decisive starting point of modern British drama and the policy created a new generation of British playwrights. The first wave included John Osborne, Arnold Wesker, John Arden, Ann Jellicoe, N F Simpson and Edward Bond. Early seasons included new international plays by Bertolt Brecht, Eugène Ionesco, Samuel Beckett, Jean-Paul Sartre and Marguerite Duras.

The theatre started with the 400-seat proscenium arch Theatre Downstairs, and in 1969 opened a second theatre, the 60-seat studio Theatre Upstairs. Some productions transfer to the West End, such as Terry Johnson's Hitchcock Blonde, Caryl Churchill's Far Away and Conor McPherson's The Weir. Recent touring productions include Sarah Kane's 4.48 Psychosis (US tour) and Ché Walker's Flesh Wound (Galway Arts Festival). The Royal Court also co-produces plays which have transferred to the West End or toured internationally, such as Conor McPherson's Shining City (with Gate Theatre, Dublin), Sebastian Barry's The Steward of Christendom and Mark Ravenhill's Shopping and Fucking (with Out of Joint), Martin McDonagh's The Beauty Queen Of Leenane (with Druid), Ayub Khan Din's East is East (with Tamasha).

Since 1994 the Royal Court's artistic policy has again been vigorously directed to finding and producing a new generation of playwrights. The writers include Joe Penhall, Rebecca Prichard, Michael Wynne, Nick Grosso, Judy Upton, Meredith Oakes, Sarah Kane, Anthony Neilson, Judith Johnson, James Stock, Jez Butterworth, Marina Carr, Phyllis Nagy, Simon Block, Martin McDonagh, Mark Ravenhill, Ayub Khan Din, Tamantha Hammerschlag, Jess Walters, Ché Walker, Conor McPherson, Simon Stephens, Richard Bean, Roy Williams, Gary Mitchell, Mick Mahoney, Rebecca Gilman, Christopher Shinn, Kia Corthron, David Gieselmann, Marius von Mayenburg, David Eldridge, Leo Butler, Zinnie Harris, Grae Cleugh, Roland Schimmelpfennig, Chloe Moss, DeObia Oparei, Enda Walsh, Vassily Sigarev, the Presnyakov Brothers, Marcos Barbosa, Lucy Prebble, John Donnelly, Clare Pollard, Robin French, Elyzabeth Gregory Wilder, Rob Evans, Laura Wade and Debbie Tucker Green. This expanded programme of new plays has been made possible through the support of A.S.K. Theater Projects and the Skirball Foundation, The Jerwood Charity, the American Friends of the Royal Court Theatre and (in 1994/5 and 1999) in association with the National Theatre Studio.

In recent years there have been record-breaking productions at the box office, with capacity houses for Joe Penhall's Dumb Show, Conor McPherson's Shining City, Roy Williams' Fallout and Terry Johnson's Hitchcock Blonde.

The refurbished theatre in Sloane Square opened in February 2000, with a policy still inspired by the first artistic director George Devine. The Royal Court is an international theatre for new plays and new playwrights, and the work shapes contemporary drama in Britain and overseas.

# AWARDS FOR ROYAL COURT

Jez Butterworth won the 1995 George Devine Award, the Writers' Guild New Writer of the Year Award, the Evening Standard Award for Most Promising Playwright and the Olivier Award for Best Comedy for Mojo.

The Royal Court was the overall winner of the 1995 Prudential Award for the Arts for creativity, excellence, innovation and accessibility. The Royal Court Theatre Upstairs won the 1995 Peter Brook Empty Space Award for innovation and excellence in theatre.

Michael Wynne won the 1996 Meyer-Whitworth Award for The Knocky. Martin McDonagh won the 1996 George Devine Award, the 1996 Writers' Guild Best Fringe Play Award, the 1996 Critics' Circle Award and the 1996 Evening Standard Award for Most Promising Playwright for The Beauty Queen of Leenane. Marina Carr won the 19th Susan Smith Blackburn Prize (1996/7) for Portia Coughlan. Conor McPherson won the 1997 George Devine Award, the 1997 Critics' Circle Award and the 1997 Evening Standard Award for Most Promising Playwright for The Weir. Ayub Khan Din won the 1997 Writers' Guild Awards for Best West End Play and New Writer of the Year and the 1996 John Whiting Award for East is East (co-production with Tamasha).

Martin McDonagh's The Beauty Queen of Leenane (co-production with Druid Theatre Company) won four 1998 Tony Awards including Garry Hynes for Best Director. Eugene Ionesco's The Chairs (co-production with Theatre de Complicite) was nominated for six Tony awards. David Hare won the 1998 Time Out Live Award for Outstanding Achievement and six awards in New York including the Drama League, Drama Desk and New York Critics Circle Award for Via Dolorosa. Sarah Kane won the 1998 Arts Foundation Fellowship in Playwriting. Rebecca Prichard won the 1998 Critics' Circle Award for Most Promising Playwright for Yard Gal (co-production with Clean Break).

Conor McPherson won the 1999 Olivier Award for Best New Play for The Weir. The Royal Court won the 1999 ITI Award for Excellence in International Theatre. Sarah Kane's Cleansed was judged Best Foreign Language Play in 1999 by Theater Heute in Germany. Gary Mitchell won the 1999 Pearson Best Play Award for Trust. Rebecca Gilman was joint winner of the 1999 George Devine Award and won the 1999 Evening Standard Award for Most Promising Playwright for The Glory of Living.

In 1999, the Royal Court won the European theatre prize New Theatrical Realities, presented at Taormina Arte in Sicily, for its efforts in recent years in discovering and producing the work of young British dramatists.

Roy Williams and Gary Mitchell were joint winners of the George Devine Award 2000 for Most Promising Playwright for Lift Off and The Force of Change respectively. At the Barclays Theatre Awards 2000 presented by the TMA, Richard Wilson won the Best Director Award for David Gieselmann's Mr Kolpert and Jeremy Herbert won the Best Designer Award for Sarah Kane's 4.48 Psychosis. Gary Mitchell won the Evening Standard's Charles Wintour Award 2000 for Most Promising Playwright for The Force of Change. Stephen Jeffreys' I Just Stopped by to See the Man won an AT&T: On Stage Award 2000.

David Eldridge's Under the Blue Sky won the Time Out Live Award 2001 for Best New Play in the West End. Leo Butler won the George Devine Award 2001 for Most Promising Playwright for Redundant. Roy Williams won the Evening Standard's Charles Wintour Award 2001 for Most Promising Playwright for Clubland. Grae Cleugh won the 2001 Olivier Award for Most Promising Playwright for Fucking Games. Richard Bean was joint winner of the George Devine Award 2002 for Most Promising Playwright for Under the Whaleback. Caryl Churchill won the 2002 Evening Standard Award for Best New Play for A Number. Vassily Sigarev won the 2002 Evening Standard Charles Wintour Award for Most Promising Playwright for Plasticine. Ian MacNeil won the 2002 Evening Standard Award for Best Design for A Number and Plasticine. Peter Gill won the 2002 Critics' Circle Award for Best New Play for The York Realist (English Touring Theatre). Ché Walker won the 2003 George Devine Award for Most Promising Playwright for Flesh Wound. Lucy Prebble won the 2003 Critics' Circle Award and the 2004 George Devine Award for Most Promising Playwright, and the TMA Theatre Award 2004 for Best New Play for The Sugar Syndrome. Linda Bassett won the 2004 TMA Theatre Award for Best Actress (for Leo Butler's Lucky Dog). Laura Wade was joint winner of the George Devine Award 2005 for Breathing Corpses.

# ROYAL COURT BOOKSHOP

The Royal Court bookshop offers a range of contemporary plays and publications on the theory and practice of modern drama. The staff specialise in assisting with the selection of audition monologues and scenes.
Many Royal Court playtexts from past and present productions cost £2.
The Bookshop is situated in the downstairs ROYAL COURT BAR AND FOOD.
Monday–Friday 3–10pm, Saturday 2.30–10pm
For information tel: 020 7565 5024
or email: bookshop@royalcourttheatre.com

## PROGRAMME SUPPORTERS

The Royal Court (English Stage Company Ltd) receives its principal funding from Arts Council England, London. It is also supported financially by a wide range of private companies, charitable and public bodies, and earns the remainder of its income from the box office and its own trading activities.

The Genesis Foundation supports International Playwrights and the Young Writers' Festival. The Jerwood Charity supports new plays by new playwrights through the Jerwood New Playwrights series.

The Skirball Foundation funds a Playwrights' Programme at the theatre. The Artistic Director's Chair is supported by a lead grant from The Peter Jay Sharp Foundation, contributing to the activities of the Artistic Director's office. Bloomberg Mondays, the Royal Court's reduced price ticket scheme, is supported by Bloomberg. Over the past eight years the BBC has supported the Gerald Chapman Fund for directors.

# ROYAL COURT
## SLOANE SQUARE

11–29 October
**Jerwood Theatre Downstairs**

# MY NAME IS RACHEL CORRIE

Taken from the writings of Rachel Corrie
Edited by **Alan Rickman** and **Katharine Viner**

director **Alan Rickman**
design **Hildegard Bechtler**
lighting design **Johanna Town**
sound design **Emma Laxton**

cast **Megan Dodds**

**MY NAME IS RACHEL CORRIE** has been developed in collaboration with the Royal Court International Department with the kind permission of Rachel Corrie's family

8 September–1 October
**Jerwood Theatre Upstairs**

# FEWER EMERGENCIES
by **Martin Crimp**

director **James Macdonald**
design **Tom Pye**
lighting design **Martin Richman**
sound design **Ian Dickinson**
composer **Mel Mercier**

cast: **Rachael Blake,
Neil Dudgeon, Paul Hickey,
Tanya Moodie**

FEWER EMERGENCIES is supported by the Royal Court's PRODUCTION SYNDICATE

**BOX OFFICE
020 7565 5000
BOOK ONLINE
www.royalcourttheatre.com**

# Harvest

# Acknowledgements

I would like to thank Sean Holmes, Chris Campbell, Ian Rickson, Graham Whybrow, Karen Douglas, Paul Miller, Dinah Wood, Wilson Milam, and Richard Wilson for reading the early drafts of the script.

I was helped in the research by my mother and father; former pig farmers John and Gwen Hart; and the veterinary Simon Cherry.

*RB*

'God made the country – man made the town.'

*Virgil  (70 – 19 BC)*

# Characters

### 1914: THE STALLION MAN
WILLIAM • ALBERT • MAM • PARKER

### 1934: ADAM AND EVE
MAUDIE • ALBERT • WILLIAM •
LORD PRIMROSE AGAR

### 1944: THE NAZI
LAURA • STEFAN • WILLIAM • MAUDIE •
ALBERT • LORD PRIMROSE AGAR •
WARCLIFFE • WAC OFFICER

### 1958: MUCK DAY
WILLIAM • MAUDIE • LAURA • STEFAN •
LORD PRIMROSE AGAR

### 1979: A ROMAN ROAD
ALAN • TITCH • LAURA • STEFAN •
WILLIAM

### 1995: SUFFRAGETTE
WILLIAM • LAURA • VET • TITCH

### 2005: A SONG IN YOUR HEART
DANNY • BLUE • LAURA • LEWIS •
YOUNG AGAR • WILLIAM

# 1914

# The Stallion Man

*1914 August. Mid-morning. The big farmhouse table is set running from stage left to stage right. Enter WILLIAM. He is 19, and handsome with refined features. He is dusty from the harvest, and wears sacking around his legs which has become wet. He runs upstairs, and once in his room takes a letter from his trousers, reads it and then hides it. He runs downstairs.* suspence!

*As he is halfway down the stairs ALBERT enters. He is 18, WILLIAM's brother, and broader with rougher features. He is also dusty, with the same sacking on the legs. ALBERT looks at WILLIAM suspiciously. ALBERT quenches his thirst from a jug of water. He is rough and functional in his manners.*

**William**  'ot.

**Albert**  Aye.

*WILLIAM quenches his thirst using a cup.*

Where d'yer go on yer 'lowance?

**William**  Mind yer own.

**Albert**  Spittle Garth meadow?

**William**  Mebbe. Mebbe not.

*WILLIAM pours some stew from a pot, cuts some bread, sits and begins to eat.*

**Albert**  He found out worr it was.

**William**  Aye?

**Albert**  Aye.

*ALBERT runs wet hands through his hair, and spits noisily into the sink. He ladles himself some stew, cuts some bread, sits and starts to eat. WILLIAM looks to ALBERT for further enlightenment but gets none.*

**William**  What worr it?

**Albert**  A vixen.

**William**  Aye?

**Albert**  Aye.

**William**  I said it worr a fox all along. I said to him, I said, 'That's the work of either one of two beasts. A fox or a Bengal Tiger.'

**Albert**  Aye?

**William**  Aye. D'he kill it?

**Albert**  Aye.

**William**  Good.

**Albert**  They say the Kaiser's gorr a withered arm.

**William**  'They say.'

**Albert**  His left arm. He can't even shek hands with it.

**William**  No-one sheks wi' the left hand. Norr even kings.

**Albert**  They've given him a little cane to carry. So he's gorr an excuse not to have to use it.

**William**  (*Impersonating the Kaiser.*) 'I vud like to help you lift zat barrel but vat vud I do vid ze cane.'

*Pause. They eat.*

The problem we've gorr is that we both wanna go. But we can't both go. Worr I'm saying is we have to find a way of deciding who's gooin. Me or you.

**Albert**  Dad's dead.

**William**  I had noticed.

*(handwritten: nice plank of information)*

**Albert**  I'm the youngest. Eldest son gets the farm. You get the farm, so you stay. All around here it's the youngest what is gooin. Sid's gooin.

*going where I've want to know*

**William**  Mad Sid or Little Sid?

**Albert**  They wouldn't have Mad Sid.

**William**  What's wrong with Mad Sid?

**Albert**  Teeth.

**William**  Aye, he's got terrible teeth. I didn't know they was choosey. So Little Sid's gooin is he?

**Albert**  Aye. He's learning hissen some French. For the girls. They eat a lot of red meat don't they, French girls. They say it meks 'em alles ready for loving.

**William**  Little Sid's an expert on French women is he? Every day he drives a cart from Driffield to Beverley and back again. When he gets adventurous, when he wakes up in the morning and thinks he's Captain Fucking Cook, he goes as far as Hull.

**Albert**  We could have a fight.

**William**  You'd win. Look, you're good with the 'osses. Most things I do, mam can do, but she don't like the 'osses over much.

**Albert**  They're onny 'osses, you don't have to like 'em. You like Brandy.

**William**  Brandy's a beautiful good natured 'oss. I an't gorr a problem with her. It's the others.

**Albert**  So what yer saying? I stay and work the farm cos I'm good with 'osses and keep it gooin so you can goo off to France and have yer fun and when you come back yer can tek it over again beein as you's the auldest.

**William**  Yer mek it sound like summat scheming. I don't see the justice in me missing out on gooin ovverseas just cos I'm twelve month aulder 'an you.

**Albert**  Worrabout your project?

**William**  This war'll all be ovver well afore the spring and spring is the right time for me project.

**Albert**  Why won't yer tell no-one worr it is?

**William**  Cos it's a bloody secret project.

**Albert**  Go on, tell us.

**William**  No, I'm not telling yer.

**Albert**  It's pigs innit?

**William**  Who towld yer?

**Albert**  Mam. I don't like pigs.

**William**  Pigs is onny mathematics. Yer not saying, 'I don't like pigs', yer saying, 'I don't like mathematics.'

**Albert**  As I see it, we both wanna go, so – [we both go and – ]

**William**  – we're gooin round the houses here.

*Pause.*

Did yer book the stallion man?

**Albert**  Aye. He's on his way through to Langtoft. He's staying there tonight. Should be here soon.

**William**  Where'd he stay last night?

**Albert**  Rudston.

**William**  Different bed every night eh. You'd like that would yer?

**Albert**  Aye. They say the stallion man has fun in about
equal measure to that stallion of his. They say he's
fathered –

**William**  – 'They say.' Who are these they?

**Albert**  You should see his clothes. He's all rigged out for
the music hall. Breeches, yellow waistcoat, bowler hat.
Like a bloody Lord. Cane with a brass knob on the end.

**William**  Aye, well we all know what that's for.

**Albert**  (*Laughing.*) Aye.

**William**  He's a nobody. He's gorr a big 'oss and the gift of
the gab. Any fool could be a stallion man. You could be
a stallion man.

**Albert**  Oh now – [come on it ain't that easy]   *? stage directions ?*

**William**  – Get yersen a big 'oss and a fancy hat. You're
good with 'osses. Then you'd get yer travel. Different
bed every night.

**Albert**  To be a proper stallion man you godda have
summat…I dunno…summat –

**William**  – indefinable.

**Albert**  Aye.

**William**  Personality.

**Albert**  Aye.

**William**  Well you an't got that.

*Brother – not said unkindly but enraging go to Albert*

(*Beat.*) Will Brandy stand for that stallion of his?

**Albert**  Aye, she's 'ot. Should be a beautiful 'oss out of our
Brandy and that big Percheron of his. Pedigree.

*setting up audience like of william*

23

*ALBERT finishes his stew and licks the plate. He then lights his pipe. WILLIAM finishes his stew, cuts himself a piece of bread and wipes his plate with the bread and eats it.*

**Albert**  Bit fancy.

**William**  I'm courting ain't I.

**Albert**  Aye, you've been behaving summat a long way off the regular all harvest.

**William**  That'll be the courting.

**Albert**  (*After a decent draw on his pipe.*) I 'ad me eye on Maudie.

**William**  We bin through this afore.

**Albert**  I thought you might go for that sister of hers.

**William**  I like Maudie. Kate's a bit of an 'andful. Why don't yer have a try at Kate?

**Albert**  (*Knowing he's no chance.*) Oh aye.

*WILLIAM lights a cigarette.*

If you're courting Maudie, you'd berrer stay, and I'll go.

**William**  We've onny just started courting.

**Albert**  (*Standing.*) I'm not courting no-one at all. That's all I'm saying. You are. And I'm the youngest. Everywhere round here it's the youngest what is gooin.

*Enter MAM carrying a dead chicken by the legs. She sticks it in a copper boiler, still holding it by the legs, and starts to count to thirty in her head.*

**William**  Stew was grand mam, ta.

**Albert**  Why yer killed that hen?

**William**  Not right, mam, eating chicken. What are we? The royal family?

**Mam**   She's stopped laying.

**William**   Tough but fair.

**Mam**   Gerrin' an egg out of her is like winter waiting for spring.

*Horses hooves are heard in the fold yard. ALBERT stands and opens the door.*

**William**   There's yer stallion man.

**Mam**   I'm not having him in the house. Not with them 'come to bed' eyes of his. (*Laughs.*)

(*To ALBERT.*) Will your Brandy stand for that stallion?

**Albert**   Aye, she's 'ot.

*ALBERT leaves closing the door behind him.*

**Mam**   What have I been hearing about you William Harrison?

**William**   I built me own spacecraft and went off to the moon. There in't nowt much up there burr a load of brambles. I filled up fifteen Kilner jars. Yer can mek yer bramble jelly now. Mek sure yer wash the dust off fost. Might be electrical.

**Mam**   You're walking out with Maudie.

**William**   That's so typical of round here, yer mek the effort of gerrin to the moon and back, without suffering a scratch, and no-one's bloody interested.

*MAM pulls the chicken out of the pan and immediately starts plucking the chicken.*

**Mam**   Language. I don't approve of you and Maudie.

**William**   Oh right then, I'll call it off.

**Mam**  Yer using Maudie to get to that sister of hers. I know you. It's Kate yer got yer eye on. I know men. I'm never wrong.

**William**  Yer wrong this time.

**Mam**  Have yer sorted out which one of yer's gooin?

**William**  As it stands we're both gooin.

**Mam**  Tut! That can't be, yer know that.

**William**  Try telling him that.

*Enter ALBERT followed by Lieutenant PARKER. PARKER is a man in his thirties in army uniform.*

**Albert**  It in't the stallion man. It's the army.

*PARKER shakes hands with everyone.*

**Parker**  Lieutenant Parker. Beautiful day, ma'am.

**Mam**  Yer requisitioning?

**Parker**  You've heard have you?

**Mam**  Aye.

**Parker**  I'll just talk you through the powers bestowed on me –

**Mam**  – We know yer powers. Just gerr on with it.

**Parker**  (*Laughs.*) I like doing business in Yorkshire. At the end of the day, when all's said and done, there's a lot of time saved, you know what I mean. Have you got your harvest in?

**William**  The corn, aye.

**Parker**  What are you, here?

**William**  Corn, barley, we're using peas as a break. Sheep. We gorr eight Holsteins an'all.

**Parker**  Holsteins?

**William**  Cows.

**Parker**  You were getting a bit technical with me there, with your 'Holsteins'. 'Cows', I've heard of. (*Laughs.*) I'm from Befnal Green, we fink milk was born in a bo'le. (*Laughs.*) Nice up this way. Wouldn't mind –

**Mam**  – It's August.

**Parker**  Yes, I can imagine.

**William**  Are you gonna take the cows?

**Parker**  We're an army, not a dairy. (*Laughs.*) What you got in the way of horses?

**William**  Six.

**Albert**  One of them's lame.

*WILLIAM glances at ALBERT. PARKER notices this.*

**Parker**  Sorry, ma'am, would you have a drink of water for a not-so-young man fighting the Germans? (*Laughs.*) It's a hot one.

**Mam**  Lemonade? I med it mesen.

**Parker**  Ooh! Smashing. We need a hundred and sixty thousand horses by next Tuesday. So far I've got seven. (*Laughs.*) And I've already come out in a rash. (*Laughs.*)

*MAM gives him a glass of lemonade. He takes a long swig.*

Marvellous. Have you two lads enlisted? My colleague, Major Caddick, is at the corn exchange in Driffield from eight tomorrow morning.

**William**  We know. We'll be there.

**Parker**  Ooh! Keen! Don't get to thinking it's automatic. There's a medical you know.

**Mam**  Onny one of 'em's gooin. Me husband's bin dead ower ten year.

**Parker**  The youngest then, that's the form.

**Albert**  That's me.

**Parker**  Anyhow, I'm not men, I'm horses. Can all your horses draw pole wagons?

**William**  Aye.

**Parker**  Lovely.

**Albert**  It don't tek long to train an 'oss up to draw a pole wagon.

**Parker**  Maybe, but we're a bit pushed for time at the moment what with the Kaiser strolling through Belgium.

**Mam**  What d'yer do if yer tek any of our 'osses?

**Parker**  You'll get a ticket. Every ticket's got a picture of the king on it.

*PARKER takes out his ticket book and flicks it.*

So you've got six horses.

**William**  We need at least a pair to keep going, for the ploughing.

**Parker**  We're not going to take them all, don't worry. The army needs feeding same as everyone.

**Albert**  We got a mare that's 'ot, she's gerrin serviced this afti. We've booked and paid for the stallion man. She's onny used for breeding. She's not been schooled to draw a pole wagon.

**Parker**  And she'll be the lame one is she?

**Albert**  Aye.

*Pause.*

**Parker**  Look son, it's not an easy job this. I try and do
it with a smile and a laugh, but at the end of the day
you're looking at the government. Your old mum,
excuse me ma'am, gave me lemonade not water. She
understands who I am, and what I can do. I can take
whatever I like, and all I have to do is give you a ticket. I
can take your cows, your pigs, your chickens, your pole
wagons, your salt and pepper pots, (*Laughs.*) your doors,
your wallpaper, your walls. So don't start getting clever
with me son, because it's not even lunchtime yet and
I've got a full book of tickets. Your brother here said 'all'
your horses can draw a pole wagon. All. Let's go have a
look at the beauties, eh.

*ALBERT and PARKER leave, closing the door behind
him.*

**Mam**  He'll leave us a pair.

**William**  Aye, Bess and that auld bastard Punch.

**Mam**  He'll tek one look at Brandy and that'll be that.

**William**  Aye.

**Mam**  D'yer hear him? He said the form is – it's the
youngest what goes. You're the eldest. By rights it's you
what should be staying.

**William**  Aye, well mebbe I'm tired of doin what's right.

**Mam**  Why'd'yer wanna go?

**William**  Mother, I've exhausted these fields. I'm nineteen
and I 'ant never done nowt. Seen nowt, done nowt, been
nowhere. Me whole life's been these eighty acres of
chalk and clay.

**Mam**  Yer got yer pigs.

**William**  The pigs is onny an idea.

**Mam**  This farm needs ideas.

**William**  There int nowt clever about pigs. It's nowt but mathematics.

**Mam**  Nowt difficult for you mebbe.

**William**  I'll be back afore the spring when all that starts up.

*Horses hooves are heard in the fold yard. WILLIAM goes over to the window and holds back the nets.*

**Mam**  What's he tekkin?

**William**  Venus. He's tekkin the harness an'all.

*WILLIAM lets the nets drop back.*

**Mam**  What's this with Maudie? Yer should be walking out with that sister of hers. I was hoping Albert might tek a fancy to Maudie. She's right for him, Maudie. She's plain.

**William**  I'll tell her when I see her. Mam. I like Maudie. I find Maudie calm. I find Kate alarming. Self-admiring.

**Mam**  Aye, that's why you're right for each other.

*Horses hooves are heard, and a horse's neighing. WILLIAM goes over to the window and looks through the nets.*

Saturn?

**William**  Aye.

*WILLIAM lets the nets drop again.*

**Mam**  Aye, well, they're a pair. Don't tek this the wrong way. I don't want neither of yer to go but you love, you've got Eskritt blood. Albert's gorr his father's. Don't go to the army now, let Albert go, and you can leave here when he gets back if yer must.

**William**  If dad were alive we'd both be gooin.

**Mam**  If you were truly courting Maudie you wunt want to be going. You're the eldest, no-one would blame you staying, you wunt get white feathered. Mebbe yer think gooin away will give yer that summat extra, the uniform, the glory, your absence. That summat extra to sway Katie.

**William**  It in't Katie what interests me! It's Maudie. I love Maudie!

**Mam**  Yer love her?

**William**  Aye.

**Mam**  Well, well, I never.

*WILLIAM moves over and sits at the table. He seems annoyed with the table for some reason.*

**William**  Why do we have the table like this?

**Mam**  Like what?

**William**  Running this way. It feels all wrong.

**Mam**  It's alles been there. I'm used to it.

**William**  Aye, but what I'm saying is it'd be better if we turned it round. If someone's at the sink, and someone wants to get past, it's impossible. The table's in the way. And look, there's a shadow. I'm casting a shadow.

**Mam**  Sit t'other side then.

**William**  That wouldn't feel right though would it.

*Horses hooves are heard in the fold yard.*

**Mam**  Shurrup wi' yer nonsense and go tell me what 'oss that is.

*WILLIAM goes over to the window.*

**William**  Ha! You'll never believe it, he's tekkin Punch. Ha, ha! Never mind cows he can't know nowt about 'osses neither. Ah, well, s'pose they could eat the auld bugger.

**Mam**  What's that? Three.

**William**  Aye. He's gorra leave us a pair. So he can only tek one more.

*Extended silence. WILLIAM stays watching at the window.*

**Mam**  Yer might get killed. Have you thought about that?

**William**  There's an angel for farmers.

**Mam**  That's yer dad's talk. And he's dead.

*Horses hooves are heard on the yard. WILLIAM looks over to his mother and says nothing, but lets the net curtain fall back into place. His mother goes over, pushes the curtain to one side.*

Lord God Almighty! She's a beautiful 'oss. That'll kill our Albert. They'll need hossmen. Mebbe Albert can goo with her.

*Enter ALBERT. His eyes are watering. ALBERT sits, and puts his head in his hands.*

**William**  Is he done? He's leaving us a pair is he?

*ALBERT doesn't answer. Enter PARKER.*

**Parker**  All done. Everything tickety boo.

*He starts writing out tickets on the kitchen table. Still standing. He glances at ALBERT.*

I've taken four horses ma'am and four sets of harness. I've left you a good pair for your ploughing.

*He stamps the ticket. When he finishes a ticket he stamps it with a government stamp.*

Shire mare. Venus.

*He stamps the ticket.*

Shire mare. Saturn.

*He stamps the ticket.*

(*Doubtful.*) Clydesdale gelding. Punch. He's a bit old. Alright is he?

**William** Punch? Aye, he's a smashing 'oss. He'll win the war for yer.

**Parker** (*Doubtful.*) Lovely. Right.

*PARKER stamps the ticket.*

Percheron mare. She's a beauty. Kaw! Have you ever showed her?

**William** Aye. She's won a couple.

**Parker** Not surprised. Lovely looking horse. What d'yer call her? He wouldn't tell me.

**William** Brandy.

**Parker** Brandy? Lovely! It's that dapple grey isn't it. (*Laughs.*)

*ALBERT starts sobbing.*

If I had a penny for every shilling I'd put on a grey, I'd be laughing. (*Laughs.*)

**Mam** You're laughing anyhow.

**Parker** Indeed.

*PARKER stamps the ticket. ALBERT is now crying. No-one attends to him.*

After this war is won, if she comes back, you can tear up the tickets, if she don't come back, them'll be worth something. Good day to you ma'am.

*PARKER gives the tickets to MAM. They all listen to ALBERT crying.*

If it's any use to you, seeing as how one of your lads has to stay on the farm – and I can say this because I know war Mrs Harrison, I was in South Africa and I saw a few things that I can only describe as impolite – on behalf of Major Caddick, God and the King, in that order – that lad of yours there is a fine strapping lad, but he's no use to us.

*PARKER exits closing the door behind him. ALBERT continues his sobbing. MAM looks over to WILLIAM who looks away.*

*To black.*

# 1934
# Adam and Eve

*1934. March. Early evening, and not yet dark. The farmhouse kitchen. Enter MAUDIE, she is carrying a freshly killed rabbit. She hangs the rabbit on a nail from a beam and swiftly pulls down on the rabbit's fur and skins it completely in one go. She unhooks the rabbit and begins to prepare it. Enter ALBERT with a shotgun. He goes to the gun cabinet to get more cartridges.*

**Maudie**  Cawld.

**Albert**  Aye.

**Maudie**  How many more have yer lost then?

**Albert**  Tither.

**Maudie**  What were you doing? Sleeping? That's more than one fox then. You don't lose three lambs to the one fox.

**Albert**  Aye.

**Maudie**  Yer wanna tek William up there with you. He'd be alright in the hut.

**Albert**  I don't want him up theere with me. *criticizing of Albert*

**Maudie**  He's gorra good eye. He can handle a rifle, he's had the training. You can't hit a barn door at ten paces.

**Albert**  I don't want his rifle and I don't want his company.

(*Beat.*) Did he do it? What he said he was gonna do?

**Maudie**  Aye. *suspense*

**Albert**  Oh bugger. Has the squire bin round?

**Maudie**  Not yet.

*Enter WILLIAM. He is in a wheelchair which is a comfy chair set on a bogie of pram wheels. He has lost both legs. He has with him stashed in his chair a pad of paper, a book, and a newspaper, a scarf, a hat. The chair is more a 'station' than a chair. He smokes a pipe.*

**Albert**  What you bin doing?

**William**  Chasing rabbits. *suspense*

**Albert**  I've heard what you done. Did anyone see yer?

**William**  Aye. It'll be all round Yorkshire bi now. Bin losing lambs?

**Albert**  Aye.

**Maudie**  There's no use offering, he don't want yer company.

**William**  I promise to do everything in me powers not to gerr on yer nerves.

I'll not talk, I won't sing, and I'll mek a particular effort not to mention them grunty things.

*MAUDIE laughs.*

**Albert**  I'm not gerrin' into pigs and that's final.

**William**  Maudie! Did I say pigs?!

**Albert**  (*To MAUDIE.*) You're my wife! Mark whose side yer on.

(*To WILLIAM.*) Round here's too cawld for pigs. Yer know what Grandad Harrison used to say.

**Maudie**  'A cawld pig is a thin pig.'

**William**  'Do you Edward Herbert Harrison take this woman to be your lawful wedded wife?' 'A cawld pig is a thin pig!'

**Maudie**  (*Laughs.*) Shush!

**Albert**  Pigs are the worst bloody mothers on the ark.

**Maudie**  (*To WILLIAM.*) You can't deny that!

**William**  Bulls have horns, ducks quack, pigs are lousy mothers. Fact. House them indoors, manage the farrowing, and separate the sow from the litter. Pigs is a better bet than milk. We ant gorr enough land to build up a dairy herd.

**Albert**  We gorr enough grazing for sixty head. And we can buy in cattle cake.

**William**  The milking parlour onny teks twennie.

**Maudie**  (*To WILLIAM.*) He wants to borrow money.

**William**  Oh aye.

**Albert**  I'm limited by the size of the parlour.

**William**  How come I ant heard mention of this?

**Maudie**  He tawld me not to tell yer.

**Albert**  Maudie!

**William**  Borrowing money? Kaw! What a terrible, terrible thing auld grandad Harrison did to us all when he won that bloody wager.

**Albert**  It's the right size farm this, for a family farm.

**William**  Eighty acres of up and down!? It's exactly the wrong size farm. Too small to tek owt to market, and just big enough so's it's full time working. I'll tell yer the right size family farm – the squire's. Forty thousand fucking acre.

**Maudie**  Language!

**William**  Stuck here with you two. With my army training I coulda gone to Canada and bin a mountie.

**Albert**  They'd never have tekken yer.

**William**  Yer don't need legs. Yer gerr an 'oss. Canada, aye. Find mesen a little squaw. Cabin – log cabin. Fire – log fire. Dog – log dog.

**Maudie**  (*Laughs.*) Stop it!

**William**  Some decent huts is all we need. I've done a design for a pig house with… [separate stalls for the sows…]

**Albert**  (*Banging the gun on the table.*) I'm not gerrin into pigs!

*Silence.*

**Maudie**  Put that gun away. Things are bad enough without the squire opening the door and seeing you prepared for Armageddon.

*ALBERT complies.*

Eh, worr am I gonna do? I ant gorr owt to offer him.

**William**  Everything we got was his once anyhow.

**Albert**  Got some whisky ant we?

**William**  He's a cannibal. Offer him human flesh. An ear.

**Maudie**  Don't you go mentioning that cannibalism business when he's in my kitchen or I'll kill yer!

**Albert**  Anyone stranded like that with all the food gone, would do what he did. The Lord'll forgive him. Any road, don't exaggerate, it was onny an eskimo, and she were already dead.

**William**  Mebbe the squire'll sign yer book for yer.

**Albert**  Aye. It might gerr us off on the right foot an'all.

*ALBERT picks the book off the sideboard.*

My favourite bit is when the son has to dig his father's grave to teach him the dignity of labour. That's not a bad idea that.

**William**  It's all med up. Rescued by eskimos, teks seven wives, has twenty-four children, and teaches them all to yodel.

**Albert**  Forget his story, you'd better have your story straight for him.

**William**  I'm gonna the pub.

**Albert**  You're not gooin nowhere! This is your doing!

**William**  He's not the bloody king you know. He's a bloody headcase.

**Albert**  Sh!

*The sound of a dog barking at someone's arrival.*

(*Standing and listening.*) That's the squire.

*More barking.*

**William**  No, no, no. That's a dog.

*MAUDIE laughs. ALBERT has opened the door, stepped through into the fold yard.*

**Albert**  (*Off.*) Evening sir.

**William**  (*With contempt.*) Sir.

**Maudie**  (*To WILLIAM.*) You behave!

**Agar**  (*Off.*) Who are you?

**Albert**  (*Off.*) Albert Harrison sir. Put yer stick ower theere if –

**Agar**  (*Off, snapping.*) No!

**Maudie**  (*Quietly.*) Oh bloody hell.

*Enter AGAR and ALBERT. AGAR is a man of about 25. He's dressed in shorts and a vest over which he wears a full length coat made out of bear skins. He has a stout staff on which is drawn and carved many weird ethnic things suggestive of Native American or Innuit cultures. His hair is in a pony tail.*

**Agar**  (*Shaking hands with MAUDIE.*) Who are you?

**Maudie**  Mrs Harrison sir.

**William**  Maudie.

**Agar**  Is that long for Maud?

**Maudie**  Yes. How are yer sir?

**Agar**  I don't know.

*AGAR shakes hands with WILLIAM.*

William isn't it? I remember you! It's the wheels! Albert Harrison, Maudie Harrison, and William Harrison. And who is married to whom?

**Albert**  I'm married to Maudie sir.

**Agar**  Good. And you two, the two men, are you brothers?

**Albert**  Aye.

**Agar**  Yes, that's often the way.

(*To WILLIAM.*) And are you married William?

**William**  No.

**Agar**  (*To ALBERT.*) Do you have a son?

**Albert**  No.

**Agar**  Daughter?

**Albert**  No.

**Agar**  No?

**Albert**  No.

**Agar**  Do you have a chair?

**Maudie**  Yes, sorry sir.

*MAUDIE gives him a chair. He sits. Holding his stick in front of him.*

**Agar**  (*Looking at the ground.*) It's very sad this. Indicative of a greater malaise. People.

**Maudie**  Would you like a glass of whisky sir?

**Agar**  Yes.

*MAUDIE pours a glass of whisky. ALBERT gives the book to AGAR.*

**Albert**  I knows it's not what brings you here sir, burr I wonder if you wunt mind signing yer book for us.

*AGAR signs the book.*

**William**  I think the title skews it towards being summat that it int.

**Agar**  Concur. I wanted to call it 'Living with the Innuit. The Incredible Arctic Circle Adventures of Lord Primrose Agar – As told by himself in his own words.' They said that's too long.

**William**  Their title's certainly shorter. 'Cannibal!'

**Agar**  Have you read the book Maudie?

**Maudie**  Yes, I thought it were very good, sir. Exciting. It's a wonder you're still alive, what with all them women slowing you down.

**Agar**  It's a man's book really. My brother often mentions you William. Ypres. (*Pronounced correctly, i.e. Eepres.*)

**William**  The officers were at Eepres, I was at Wipers. How is he?

**Agar**  Not well. How do you manage without legs William?

**William**  Banjo.

**Maudie**  That's his pony sir.

**Agar**  Ah!

**Albert**  This new German fellah looks like a bit of a rum un.

**Agar**  (*Mimes putting ingredients into a mixing bowl and mixing them.*) Socialism. Nationalism. Sentimentality. (*He makes the sound of an explosion.*)

41

**Maudie**  Aye, well war's always good for cereal prices.

**Albert**  Onny time we int swamped by imports eh!

**William**  That hunt of yours in't doing much good round Kilham top.

**Agar**  Losing lambs eh?

**Albert**  I'll spend the night in the hut again with the gun.

**Agar**  It's a wonderful thing for a man isn't it. A night in a hut.

**Albert**  Aye. I bin up there all day.

**Agar**  What did you say?

**Albert**  I've been up there all day sir. In the hut.

*AGAR frowns, puzzled, finishes his whisky, and claps his hands.*

(*To WILLIAM.*) What have you done with my dairy herd?

**William**  I took 'em all to Scarborough for the day out. You shoulda seen their little faces. None of them had ever seen the ocean.

**Agar**  Where are they?

**William**  Where's our rent for the field?

*WILLIAM picks out a diary from the side of the chair and reads from it.*

October, no rent, spoke to Sammy Ellwood, he ses, 'I'll talk to the young squire.' November, no rent, spoke to Sammy, 'I'll talk to the young squire.' December, no rent. Rode up to the house, asked to speak to the young squire, tawld he was in London meeting his publishers. February, no rent, spoke to Sammy Ellwood, he said to me – 'fuck off you'.

**Agar**  I'll have a word with Mr Ellwood.

**William**  Five months rent. Five shillings. Pay up and I'll tell yer where I've put yer cows.

*AGAR counts out five shillings. He makes to give the money to WILLIAM.*

Maudie's in charge of money.

*MAUDIE takes it, counts it, and nods approval to WILLIAM.*

Yer cows are at Fimber. Rogersons. I don't understand yer mentality. Yer've got forty thousand acres across Yorkshire but yer choose to rent a field from us. It in't cos yer need to rent, it's cos yer want the field. If yer had a scheme to tek our best grazing and not pay us and thereby bust us it ain't gonna work. Yer grandad lost Kilham Wold Farm in a bet, fair and square, it's all legal, I seen the mandate in writing.

**Agar**  My grandfather had a character flaw.

**William**  He was a drunk and a gambler. And worst of all a loser.

**Albert**  We're not for sale sir. We're doing alright. We gerr a monthly milk cheque. I'm thinking very long term.

*AGAR stands and makes to go.*

**Agar**  You don't have a son.

*Pause.*

Did you buy anything today in Beverley? At the farm sale?

**Albert**  A cake crusher.

**Agar**  I thought I'd seen you there. You looked right through me. (*Stands.*) Pappachakwoquai! Innuit for

43

'may your ancestors walk beside you'. Goodnight Mrs Harrison.

**Maudie**  Goodnight sir.

**William**  If this farm were still in the estate, what would you be doing on it?

**Agar**  Pigs.

*AGAR and ALBERT leave. ALBERT closes the door behind him.*

**Maudie**  You had no right to talk to him like that! Ever since you come back from abroad you bin as lippy as I don't know what.

**William**  Abroad? I dint go on the grand tour you know.

*Enter ALBERT.*

**Maudie**  (*To ALBERT.*) What the bloody hell's this about Beverley?

**Albert**  I went to a farm sale.

**Maudie**  You told me you were up on the tops! You lied to me Albert Harrison!

**Albert**  I went to Beverley to a farm sale to try and pick up a cake crusher.

**Maudie**  We've already gorr a cake crusher!

**Albert**  It's on its last legs.

**Maudie**  I found yer a second-hand cake crusher onny a minute down the road.

**Albert**  It's onny Beverley I an't bin to bloody London.

**Maudie**  Stop cursing in my kitchen! So you went to Beverley to gerr a cake crusher?

**Albert**  Aye.

**William**  So did you get one then?

**Albert**  Aye. I gorr a couple.

**Maudie**  Two!?

**William**  Why d'yer buy two?

**Albert**  It was a bargain. The second one.

**Maudie**  Why dint yer just buy the second one then?

**Albert**  I'd already bought the fost one.

**William**  That's three bloody cake crushers we got now!

**Maudie**  We've onny got twennie-five head of cattle! We've hardly need of one cake crusher!

**William**  If you buy the cake crusher down the road we'll have four!

**Maudie**  There's farm sales every week by the end of the month we could have a dozen cake crushers!

**William**  Start a cake crusher museum.

**Albert**  (*He bangs the gun on the table.*) We needed a cake crusher! I went to Beverley and got one.

*Pause.*

**William**  Two.

*MAUDIE laughs.*

Don't gerr him mardy, he's gorra gun in his hand.

**Maudie**  You're up to summat!

**Albert**  (*To MAUDIE.*) You! Leave us a minute.

**Maudie**  No! If it's farm talk I'm having some of it.

**Albert**  It's not farm talk! It's brothers! You're my wife! Leave us be for a while.

**William**  Go on love, go and give yer chickens a bollocking.

**Maudie**  Aye, I will, might gerr a bit of respect.

*She slams the door behind her. ALBERT struggles and fiddles. WILLIAM lets him struggle.*

**William**  Some women, I've heard, do what yer tell 'em without any fuss.

*Pause.*

You wan't on the tops then today?

**Albert**  I paid Mad Sid to sit in the hut. Burr he's very badly at the moment.

**William**  Who's he think he is today?

**Albert**  Beryl Carter.

**William**  Never heard of her.

**Albert**  Must be some lass he knows from Brid. I've done some wrong, some evil. Don't tell Maudie will yer?

**William**  You bin to see a tart in Beverley?

**Albert**  No. I dint go straight to the farm sale. I went up to the hospital.

**William**  Yer what?

**Albert**  Aye, I climbed ovver the 'ospital fence, went through the gardens. I knew where to go cos that's where Katie had her little Laura. There was a side door open and I went in and it's just after dinner time and I teks me hat off, and smiles at the mothers like I'm a dad, and I just have to gerrout cos I can feel me face just burning up, and I'm in a corridor and there's a side room and I can see there's a bain in theere and the mother's asleep. Little lass, couldn't be more than sixteen, bonny but summat common about her. Mebbe she wan't wed and that's why she were in that room, I dunno. I have a look see if the bain is a boy. He is. I pick him up and he dunt cry or owt. I walk out.

**William**  Get yersen a drink.

*ALBERT stands and pours himself a whisky, then sits.*

Don't worry about me.

**Albert**  Aye. Sorry.

*ALBERT stands and pours a drink for WILLIAM. Then sits and drinks.*

Never been one for this stuff. It's alright. I picked the bain out the cot…and headed straight out across the gardens with 'im. I gorr half way across and there's this nurse, a sister I think, bit aulder, sitting on a bench and she stands and ses, 'Hello.' Just like that. 'Hello.' And I ses, 'How do?' – and she ses, 'D'yer want me to tek that bain off yer hands?' and I ses, 'Aye,' and I gives her the little bugger and she looks at me and it was like them auld eyes of hers is looking deep down into my soul, and me face is burning up again, and I climb the fence and I run to the hoss and I'm away.

*ALBERT drinks.*

I can see why some folk can get accustomed to this stuff.

*He tops up his drink, and drinks again.*

He was a fine, dark looking boy, despite his mother. I think he woulda ended up being a good, big lad. Aye, well. I don't think she was a country lass though. She'd be Beverley or Hull mebbe.

**William**  Yer picked a bain up, walked ten yards, and give it to a nurse.

**Albert**  The Good Lord's seen everything.

**William**   Yer intent was badly wrong, but at the end of the day, when all's said and done, the world is the same today, as it was yesterday.

**Albert**   Fastest way of losing this land is having no-one to work it.

**William**   That's beyond argument.

**Albert**   That's what the squire was talking about. 'You ain't gorr a son.' Did yer heard him?

**William**   They cut me legs off Albert, not me ears.

**Albert**   There int no more Harrisons.

**William**   There's Laura.

**Albert**   (*As if it's been said before.*) She's not an Harrison.

**William**   She's our niece. She's fifteen now and is still showing a liking for the life. She's up from Hull every holiday. (*Pause.*) Are yer still doing it?

**Albert**   There dunt seem no reason no more. She bin fifteen years wi me and she ant bin nowhere near carrying. I think the Lord has seen fit to punish me for my sinning as a young man.

**William**   Maudie might be barren.

**Albert**   I can feel the sin within me. The Lord gave me Maudie, when by rights she was yourn. I'm in the same position as Adam's brother.

**William**   Adam who?

**Albert**   Adam and Eve.

**William**   He didn't have a brother.

**Albert**   That's my point. Mebbe he did, but if the brother din't have a son he wouldn't gerr in the story, d'yer see? We need a son. Do yer understand worr I'm saying?

**William**  I do.

**Albert**  Sometimes I wish Grandad Harrison hadn't med that wager with the Squire. He's med a rod for the back of every Harrison following him. You know worr I'm asking don't yer?

**William**  Aye.

*ALBERT stands and picks up the shotgun.*

**Albert**  Yer loved her once. I'm off up the tops.

**William**  Tek the rifle.

*ALBERT swaps the shotgun for the rifle.*

You won't have spoken to Maudie then?

**Albert**  No. I thought I'd leave that one to you.

*ALBERT leaves taking the rifle. WILLIAM sits and thinks. There is the hint of a smile. Enter MAUDIE.*

**Maudie**  Ha! He's tekken the rifle then eh?

**William**  Aye.

**Maudie**  How much did you drink in the end?

**William**  The fox'll be safe purr it that way.

**Maudie**  What are you looking at?

**William**  You.

**Maudie**  You're terrible you.

**William**  Aye. You make me terrible.

**Maudie**  Shh!

**William**  I like lambing time. Every year I like lambing more and more.

**Maudie**  He might not be gone.

*She checks by looking through the window.*

**William**  Do you like lambing?

*She kisses him on the top of the head.*

**Maudie**  It's me favourite time of the whole year.

*To black.*

# 1944
# The Nazi

*1944. April. Afternoon, still light, but beginning to fade. The nets are covered with blackout curtains, open. A wireless sits on the sideboard. LAURA sits up in bed. She is aged about 25 and dressed in farm gear.*

**Laura**  Do all Germans fuck like that?

*STEFAN sits up. He is a young German of about 25.*

**Stefan**  Only the Luftwaffe.

*They kiss. They both begin to dress. She in overalls and he in Prisoner of War issue overalls with a big yellow circle on the back.*

Laura, I want to sleep here tonight. In this bed.

**Laura**  Don't be daft!

**Stefan**  I will go back to the camp, sign in, and sneak out when it is dark.

**Laura**  They'll shoot yer.

**Stefan**  In two years now they have shot no-one.

**Laura**  No. Worr I meant is – Uncle Albert'll shoot yer.

**Stefan**  Why doesn't he like me Laura?

**Laura**  You're German, and we're at war with Germany.

**Stefan**  Ah, I see. Is that it do you think?

*STEFAN snuggles up to her.*

**Laura**  He wun't shoot yer just cos yer German, but a German fucking his niece in his house – then he'd not go looking for any other excuses. Everything's black and white for Uncle Albert. He never liked me mam, so he dunt like me. Uncle Will likes yer.

**Stefan**  You smell of paraffin. Nothing, even if I live to be a hundred and ten will smell more beautiful than paraffin.

**Laura**  Who in their right mind would wanna live to an hundred and ten?

**Stefan**  Anyone who is a hundred and nine.

*They go downstairs.*

**Laura**  My great Uncle Tom lived to one hundred and seven.

**Stefan**  So that's true then?! Uncle Will told me he won the farm in a bet. He wagered the squire that he would live longer than the squire's dog?

**Laura**  They had a legal mandate drawn up. The dog was a puppy and Great Uncle Tom was ninety-four.

*They kiss. He undoes her top. The drone of a low flying aircraft approaching. STEFAN dives under the table.*

**Stefan**  Heinkel... H E One-eleven. Laura!

*LAURA goes to the doorway. She undoes her top and shows her brassiered bust to the aircraft as it roars overhead. She laughs.*

**Laura**  He's waving! Ha, ha!

*STEFAN from under the table.*

**Stefan**  Don't wave back! He'll either bomb us or land. Get under the table!

*LAURA crawls under the table. They kiss.*

**Laura**  You can't stay the night, Steffie.

**Stefan**  I am crazy for you. Like a bat in a dairy.

**Laura**  (*Laughs.*) Like a bat in a dairy? (*Laughs.*) What?

**Stefan**  Confused, lost in love. Like a bat in a dairy.

*They kiss.*

Why do they have the table here?

**Laura**  It's a kitchen table. In England the English put their kitchen tables in the kitchen.

**Stefan**  No, I mean it would obviously be better if it ran at ninety degrees to the window then the light from the window would run down the length of the table.

**Laura**  God you're lovely! Say something else like that. I love it. Makes me want you again.

**Stefan**  All I'm saying is that logically such a big table should be a utility and not an obstruction. If anyone is standing at the sink then a whole section of the room is technically closed off.

**Laura**  It's always been here, as long as I can remember. Come on.

*LAURA goes for his trousers and starts to unbutton his flies. They break as WILLIAM enters in a wheelchair.*

**William**  Haende Hoch!

**Stefan**  (*Through embarrassed laughter.*) Good afternoon. Mr Harrison.

**William**  Anyone we know?

**Laura**  We were hiding from the bomber.

**William**  Since when has hiding involved jumping up and down and flashing yer tits? I suppose yer under the table cos there's the whole committee standing around down Spittle Garth meadow. Where yer normally go.

*Looks exchanged between STEFAN and LAURA.*

I an't told no-one. That's where we used to go, in me heyday. Aye. Lovely. Grass. Get the sun on yer back.

**Stefan**  I'm sorry Mr Harrison.

*WILLIAM lights his pipe.*

**William**  Don't you dare say sorry sunshine. You're the best bloody thing ever happened round here. I wish you'd bin shot down in nineteen twenny-two.

**Stefan**  Thank you. I like the work.

**William**  British airmen in prisoner of war camps in Germany spend all their time digging tunnels and dressing up in women's clothing. I often ask myself, 'Why dunt our Stefan try and escape?'

**Stefan**  I am very happy here.

**William**  Fed and watered, and the best looking lass in Yorkshire knackering you out every time yer on yer 'lowance. Happy? Yer should be bloody delirious.

**Stefan**  I like farming.

**William**  Farming's alright if yer just wanna gerra bit involved but it's commitment that this farm needs.

**Laura**  (*To STEFAN.*) It's an old Harrison saying. Egg and bacon breakfast. The chickens are involved but the pigs are committed.

**Stefan**  I spoke to the Colonel about the huts.

**William**  Aye.

**Stefan**  He said you must know something that he doesn't. About the war being nearly over.

**William**  What's he think all these Yanks are doing legging it up and down our hills? Training for Hide and Seek. They'll soon be running up the beaches of Belgium. The Yanks have done it again. Turned up just in time to pick up all the dead men's caps. I'll buy the huts off the army if the price is right and I'll even dismantle them mesen cos Albert won't have owt to do with it.

**Laura**  How will you do that Uncle?

**William**  When I say me I mean him.

**Stefan**  You mean I'd dismantle, and…mantle those sheds all on my own?

**William**  Mantle's not a word I know about.

**Laura**  Erect.

**Stefan**  Erect?

**William**  Aye. Erect.

**Stefan**  They are very big sheds. It's not straightforward. It would be a lot of work.

**William**  I'd be paying yer then.

**Stefan**  What do you want them for?

**William**  Me secret project.

**Laura**  Pigs.

**Stefan**  Our huts are very cold in winter.

**William**  I'll double line 'em on the inside.

**Laura**  (*To STEFAN.*) You'll double line 'em on the inside.

**Stefan**  Not with wood. They chew on wood. Pigs.

**William**  I'll find summat that in't wood, that they don't like chewing on and I'll double line 'em with that.

**Laura**  (*To STEFAN.*) You'll double line 'em with that.

**William**  Anyhow, pigs is a secret project. Now listen up you two – it's gerrin ugly down there.

**Laura**  Is that the War Rag committee then?

**William**  Aye.

**Laura**  Are they gonna take the farm off us Uncle?

**William**  Norr if I can help it.

(*To STEFAN.*) I want you out the way. Any suggestion that we're not working the skin off yer back is gonna goo again us.

(*To LAURA.*) You're family. You stay in here. You're another soul they'll be mekking homeless if they boot us off the land.

*WILLIAM takes the shotgun and the rifle out of the cabinet and gives them both to STEFAN.*

(*To STEFAN.*) Get these guns out of Albert's sight. Goo up on the tops, bag us a couple of rabbits. What's the marrer?

**Stefan**  You're giving me a gun.

**Laura**  He's a Nazi.

**William**  If he's a Nazi I'm Jesse Owens. Goo on. Off yer go.

*STEFAN looks at LAURA and leaves. LAURA looks at
WILLIAM, gets a nod, and follows him out. We see STEFAN
and LAURA kissing outside. LAURA comes back in.*

**Laura**  Is that the squire then? The one in that funny coat.

**William**  Aye.

**Laura**  I can't believe they sent him to prison for writing
that book.

**William**  He med a fool of a few monied folk along the
way.

**Laura**  If they believed them stories more fool them. You
gorra be stupid to believe that someone with no training
could separate siamese twins.

**William**  He didn't separate them, they both died.

**Laura**  He never did claim they lived.

**William**  That's the trick though innit! Having 'em live.
Any idiot can separate siamese twins. D'yer love Stefan?

*LAURA starts to cry.*

Aye, it's a wonderful joyous thing is love. It's had me in
its snare in the past. Bout five times in all.

**Laura**  Who?

**William**  Yer mam.

**Laura**  Me mam!?

**William**  I was a kid and she never even noticed. I was
crazy for her.

**Laura**  Like a bat in a dairy? It's a German saying.

**William**  That's a good un. It's all radar innit, bats. In a
dairy, with all that metal about. Play havoc, wunt it. Aye.
Like a bat in a dairy for your mam I was, and never did
owt about it.

56

**Laura**  Who else? You said five.

**William**  (*Singing.*) Three madamoiselles from Armenteers, who hadn't been fucked for forty years. Inky pinky parlez-vous.

**Laura**  Uncle!

**William**  And there's another woman I can't talk about.

**Laura**  Maudie?

**William**  That'd be telling. You could marry Stefan you know. Some prisoners stayed on last time round. Henry Brown?

**Laura**  What, him what has his hair growing through his cap?

**William**  Heinrich. We'd give Stefan a job here. You're not an Harrison, and he's a fucking Hohenstaufer, burr it's the nearest we're gonna get.

**Laura**  How much of what you're saying is because Uncle Albert and Auntie Maudie don't have any children? *who*

**William**  That's the whole of it.

**Laura**  Where would we live?

**William**  My room's gonna be free soon. When I move into the barn.

**Laura**  I couldn't live here. Not with Uncle Albert.

**William**  He wunt be my first choice either. That'd be Greta Garbo but – [fat chance of that…]

**Laura**  – Uncle Albert dunt like me and he dunt like Stefan!

**William**  For a long time now I ant had much of a say in how things are done round here. But today the world is gonna change. *moves story on*

**Laura**  They can't mek us plough up Spittle Garth can they?

**William**  They took our 'osses last time. Knocked on the door, drank me mam's lemonade, and walked off with the hosses.

**Laura**  But that grass is our hay for the winter. We can't get cattle cake.

**William**  We'll have to slaughter half the herd. God knows what that'll do to Albert. People he dunt care for, burr if it stinks, shits everywhere and can't feed itsen then it pulls on his heart summat terrible.

*Enter MAUDIE.*

**Maudie**  I've never heard so much cursing! Aud Nick hissen'd be blushing.

**William**  I've heard you curse.

**Maudie**  (*Laughs.*) Onny at you. Is that pot on? He's threatening to shoot the cows in front of the committee. If he dunt shoot the cows he'll shoot the bloody committee.

**William**  Stop cursing.

**Maudie**  Am I? Bloody hell. Yer see, he's got me started.

**William**  The guns are out the house.

**Laura**  Stefan's gorr 'em both. Up on the tops.

**Maudie**  Oh good, that's a relief. We're gonna lose the farm Will. I can't gerr him to budge.

**William**  He'll see sense. We got no choice.

**Maudie**  All he's gorra do is plough that bloody field!

*Enter ALBERT.*

**William**  Where are they?

**Albert**  Gassing. Sitting in the young squire's car writin' summat up.

   (*To LAURA.*) You'd best mek yersen scarce lass.

**Maudie**  She's my sister's girl. She's family.

**Albert**  There was a time when what a man said in his own house was listened to!

**Maudie**  Yer not in your own house, yer in my kitchen!

*LAURA distributes teas.*

**Albert**  That committee is judge, jury and bloody hangman! I tell yer, if any soldier sets foot on this land I'll shoot 'em.

**William**  What with?

*ALBERT looks to the gun cabinet.*

I give the guns to Stefan. Tawld him to bag some rabbits.

**Albert**  It's tekken me thirty fuckin' year to build that herd up. Thirty fucking years! If I plough that grass, I can't feed 'em through the winter. And they bloody well know that.

*Knock on the door.*

I'm in the khazi.

*ALBERT leaves to the loo. LAURA opens the front door. Enter AGAR, followed by WARCLIFFE. AGAR is now 33 years old. He is a picture of gloom. WARCLIFFE is a scruffy, stocky Yorkshire farmer of indeterminate age.*

**Maudie**  Boots!

*They both stop and take their boots off.*

**Laura**  Would you like tea?

**Warcliffe**  We won't be ovver long.

**Maudie**  Why'd'yer tek yer boots off then?

**Warcliffe**  Milk, one sugar please love. Have yer got sugar?

**Maudie**  Mebbe! If we had sugar, you'd wanna know why we had sugar! This war's just an excuse so you can go nosing around. No! We an't gorr any sugar! Burr I might be lying! Well?!

**Warcliffe**  Milk, no sugar, please. Where's –

**Maudie**  Washing his hands.

*Silence.*

**Laura**  (*To AGAR.*) I've read your book. I think it's brilliant.

**Agar**  I made it all up. I never went to the Arctic. I spent three years in the reading room of the British Library. Near a radiator.

**Laura**  That doesn't stop it being brilliant. When Ingachook has to dig his father's grave, I thought that were great.

**Agar**  Many thanks. Are you a Harrison?

**Maudie**  Her mother's Kate, my sister. From Hull.

*A toilet flush. Enter ALBERT. WARCLIFFE looks to AGAR. AGAR nods. WARCLIFFE reads.*

**Warcliffe**  (*Reading.*) As the local Chairman of the War Agricultural Committee –

**Maudie**  (*To WARCLIFFE.*) – If you're the Chairman why are you letting him tell yer what to do?

**Warcliffe**  Lord Agar int telling me what to do.

**Maudie**  (*To AGAR.*) You looked at him and nodded as if to say 'start your talking now'.

**Agar**  I'm just another committee member Mrs Harrison.

**Warcliffe** (*To AGAR.*) Shall I carry on.

*WILLIAM and MAUDIE laugh.*

Yeah?

**Agar** Oh God. Get on with it!

**Warcliffe** Right. As the local chairman of the – [war agricultural]

**Maudie** – If you evict us, where we gonna live?

**Albert** If any soldiers step foot on my land, I'll shoot them!

**William** When does the eviction order tek effect?

**Warcliffe** Now.

**Agar** Oh God. Look. We haven't informed the army yet. The pragmatics of the situation are such that effectively you've still got two or three days. So, if I might make a suggestion, plough the bloody field.

**Albert** What is it with you and that field? This is Harrison land. Where's it say I've gorr an obligation to feed the whole of bloody England?

**Warcliffe** The Ministry of –

**Albert** Fuck the Ministry. They only want us now cos there's a war on, any other time they're happy to see us go to hell, cos they know they can get their cheap imports.

**Agar** Very true.

**Warcliffe** I issued a ploughing directive to Albert Orlando Harrison of Kilham Wold Farm with regard to seven and a half acres known as Spittle Garth –

**Albert** – them fields is me hay for the winter. That's how I'm gonna feed the herd through till next back end.

**Warcliffe** – This directive was served on the twenty-eighth of March 1944. Last Tuesday. Subsequently –

**Albert** – worr I wanna know is, how does anyone get the right to tell a man what he can and can't do on his own land.

**Warcliffe** Kilham Wold Farm was graded C by the committee, which is less than sixty percent efficient.

**Agar** Someone has decided that the country needs corn. Not meat. Not milk.

**Maudie** Why dint they get some stocks in then afore the war? They knew it was coming.

**Albert** You've gorra barn full of corn. Piled high waiting for the right price.

**Warcliffe** Lord Agar's estate's been inspected by the committee just the same as everyone else.

**Maudie** Aye, and what grade did the estate get?

**Warcliffe** Grade A.

(*To AGAR.*) Should I finish? It'll be all legal then. Yeah?

(*Reading.*) On second of April 1944, the farm was visited by the Chairman, Arnold Warcliffe, and a committee member, Lord Primrose Agar. The acres in question remained unploughed so an eviction –

*There is a knock at the door.*

Oh bloody hell!

**Laura** I'll go.

*LAURA opens the door to a Women's Auxiliary Corps officer (WAC). She is in full uniform and has a rifle slung over her shoulder.*

**WAC**  Hello. Looking for a Mr Albert Harrison, or William Harrison?

**William**  Who are you?

**WAC**  Miss Collins, Women's Auxiliary Corps. I'll be quick. This is serious. We've got instructions –

**Albert**  – Yer got no rights on this land!

**WAC**  Eh?

**William**  I don't think this is owt to do with –

**Albert**  – That's enough! I'll hear no more!

*ALBERT manhandles the WAC, which surprises her completely and he takes the rifle off her.*

**William**  Albert!

**Albert**  (*Wielding the gun at the WAC.*) Gerr ovver there!

**Maudie**  Put that bloody thing down!

**Albert**  How many's out there?

**WAC**  What the hell's – [going on]

**William**  – Albert! This has nothing –

**Albert**  (*To WILLIAM.*) I've towld you! (*To WAC.*) How many?!

**WAC**  One. Mrs Dunn. On the motorbike. She's armed. We're here –

**Albert**  – We know why you're here!

*ALBERT smashes a pane of glass in the window.*

**William**  Get down everyone!

*Everyone lies on the floor. ALBERT fires once.*

Albert! Put that thing away will yer. Yer mekking things worse.

**Albert**  Fuck off.

*ALBERT fires again.*

**William**  What have you come here for Miss Collins?!

**WAC**  (*Frightened to death.*) Report of an escaped Prisoner of War! Armed. He's been shooting off a rifle at the Americans up on the tops.

**William**  He's shooting rabbits.

*ALBERT shoots again.*

**WAC**  The Americans rang through –

*There is a crack of a rifle and the shattering of glass. ALBERT, shot through the head, slumps to the floor, dead.*

**William**  Tell your Mrs Dunn to stop firing will yer please love.

**WAC**  (*Crawling towards the door.*) Edna! Stop firing! Stop firing! Hold fire!

**William**  Tell her to shout to say she's heard yer.

**WAC**  Edna! Did you hear me!

**Mrs Dunn**  (*Off.*) Aye! I heard yer! I've stopped firing!

*They all stand.*

*Silence.*

**Maudie**  He's dead.

**William**  Aye. He is that.

*To black.*

INTERVAL

# 1958
# Muck Day

*1958. February. The farmhouse kitchen. The floor is now black and white vinyl tiles. There are signs of affluence, a fridge, a telephone. A family photo in a frame of four daughters in ascending heights. The table is still set as ever it was. WILLIAM is sat in his wheelchair writing on cards which he takes from an intricate looking colour-coded card index system. Enter MAUDIE. In work clothes, no coat.*

**Maudie**  Cawld!

**William**  Wireless ses there's penguins at Scarborough.

**Maudie**  (*Knuckling him on the head.*) Yer pulling me leg again! I tell yer what though, that shed's warm. Finishing house.

**William**  Aye, course it is.

*MAUDIE hands over six or seven coloured cards which WILLIAM takes and inspects.*

**Maudie**  Gorr a couple coughing mind. I've isolated 'em.

*Enter LAURA from outside, nine months pregnant, and walking crab-like.*

**Laura**  Chloe's ready.

**William**  'Chloe'?

**Laura**  Orange six. And blue ten, she in't in pig. Again.

**Maudie**  She's gerrin' on a bit now that one.

**William**  That's it with her then! She's going out in a pastry coffin.

**Maudie**  Are you alright?

**Laura**  I've had a little show.

**Maudie**  Oh love, yer wanna get yerself in yer room, have yer gorr a fire in there?

**Laura**  Aye, I'll go and lie down in a bit.

**Maudie**  You and yer bloody cards.

**William**  Gimme them others.

*LAURA hands over six coloured cards.*

**Laura**  Red four, green two, indigo fifteen, indigo bloody sixteen.

**William**  Have yer written the dead uns in? I ask, cos yer never do.

**Laura**  Each of them litters there has got one dead.

*WILLIAM writes in the data on the cards.*

**Maudie**  A man sitting in a warm kitchen all day, while the womenfolk gerr on wi' all the graftin'.

**William**  Shurrup yer barrel of spite! Yer used to be good fun, you did. When yer husband was still alive.

*MAUDIE knuckles him on the head.*

Ow! That's fucking twice yer've done that now!

**Maudie**  Don't curse in my kitchen!

**William**  If yer let me swear I'll marry yer.

**Maudie**  I don't want yer to marry me! I've had a change of heart.

*LAURA laughs.*

**William**  (*To MAUDIE. Offering a card.*) Go and get Chloe started. I'll send Stef in to help yer if he gets back in time.

(*To LAURA.*) You, go and have yer bath.

**Laura**  I really want to do Chloe.

**William**  Look at yer, yer can hardly stand.

**Maudie**  D'yer wann us to call Doctor Wilson?

**Laura**  Aye, well mebbe I'm exaggerating.

*MAUDIE leaves.*

**William**  We're all excited about 'Chloe'.

*LAURA goes off and turns the taps on in the bathroom.*

**Laura**  (*Off.*) I bet she has eleven!

**William**  Thirteen.

**Laura**  (*Off.*) Imagine that. Thirteen.

*The sound of a car pulling up. The horn is sounded triumphantly in a rhythm of honks.*

(*Off.*) That'll be Steffie! Has he got the car Will?!

**William**  No! He's bought the horn separate. He's gonna collect the rest of the car tomorrow.

*Enter LAURA in dressing gown, she stands in the open door looking out.*

**Laura**  Bloody hell! I'll feel like the bloody Queen sittin' up in the front of that.

**William**  Don't slip on them flags! I don't want that little lass in there starting her life with a bang on the head.

**Laura**  I wish you'd stop it with that little lass talk!

**William**  I'm willing that bain to be a boy by a convoluted method of madness which I wouldn't expect you to understand since it involves talking a lot of bollocks.

*Enter STEFAN. He kisses LAURA. STEFAN is wearing a quality tweed suit and a bow tie. He still has some German in his tongue. He carries car keys.*

**Stefan**  Are you alright?

**Laura**  Come on! Let's go for a ride!

**William**  Don't go gerrin her excited!

**Stefan**  (*To WILLIAM.*) Have you seen it?!

**William**  Shoulda put the money in new sheds.

**Stefan**  Sheds, sheds, sheds. I thought my father was a bore because all he talked about was Johann Sebastian Bach. I've swapped early baroque for pig housing.

**William**  She's had a little show.

**Stefan**  Bugger me! Really?

**Laura**  It was nowt much. Let's go to Brid!

**Stefan**  Maybe just up Fimber and back. The girls'll be home in an hour.

**Laura**  (*To WILLIAM.*) D'yer wanna come for a spin?

**William**  No. It's Thursday.

(*To STEFAN.*) Any road, you, you're busy according to this maintenance card here.

**Stefan**  Yes, I know. Sorry.

*STEFAN takes the card and reads it.*

**William**  If yer look under the fans yer'll see the asbestos has come away –

**Stefan** – I've done this already. Shed two?

**William** If yer've done it yer an't filled yer card in.

*STEFAN starts to wheel WILLIAM out the house.*

**Stefan** Come on. You'll have to show us.

**Laura** I'm in the bath.

**William** Oi, you, fill your cards in.

*LAURA picks at food from the fridge. She then sits at the pig info system and completes her cards and files them. The sound of a tractor turning up and turning off its engine. LAURA looks through the window. LAURA retreats to the bathroom. Pause. Enter AGAR. He is now a man of 45, and still gloomy. His coat and the exotic trappings of youth have gone.*

**Agar** Mr Harrison! Mr Harrison!!

*He waits. Surreptitiously he looks at the pig information system. He goes over and looks. He touches. He looks closer. Enter LAURA from stage left.*

**Laura** It's normally kept under lock and key that.

**Agar** Thursday. Again.

**Laura** Aye.

**Agar** Comes around doesn't it. It's snowing on the tops. It's actually drifting across Nafferton way.

**Laura** You might have to stay the night then.

**Agar** Oh no, I don't think so.

**Laura** I'm having a bath. Have you gorr owt for me?

**Agar** No. Not yet. I've decided to change the ending. After what you said.

**Laura** That were six month back.

**Agar**  Oh dear! Really? Time's winged chariot. Ha! I read it again and I agree with you. The denouement doesn't satisfy. It is merely morbid. I see you've got the telephone in. Maybe I could ring you.

**Laura**  No, yer can't.

*LAURA leaves for the bathroom. AGAR goes back to fiddling with the pig system, but this time he seems to understand it. Enter WILLIAM.*

**William**  Pigs! It in't nowt but mathematics. All yer need's a system.

**Agar**  Does it work?

**William**  Din't yer see that brand new Austin A90 out there?

**Agar**  I did. I've heard you're buying in straw. I could trade you straw for the muck.

**William**  Hard cash. That's the deal we have. No man on this earth can talk with any authority about happiness until he's sold shit to the aristocracy.

*WILLIAM pours a little whisky for AGAR and one for himself.*

**Agar**  I imagine you're buying in straw because you've no-one to work the arable.

**William**  I'm not selling. A farmer who sells land is like a wrestler who chops his arms off.

**Agar**  I've never heard that expression.

**William**  I just med it up. How long have we bin doing this?

**Agar**  Twenty years.

**William**  Any road, Maudie'd kill me. She likes to walk the circuit, meks her feel like a queen. I don't wanna be the Harrison who sold his inheritance and left the Harrisons with nowt to work. If I do that they'll tek me portrait off the landing and stick it in the scullery.

**Agar**  Do you have a portrait?

**William**  I thought you of all people'd spot a metaphor.

**Agar**  I don't think we've got a scullery.

*AGAR is fiddling with the pig system again.*

I've bought a small feed company. Fimber Feed.

**William**  Oh aye?

**Agar**  They've always bought my corn, and now I've bought them.

**William**  Can't see how yer can mek money out of animal feed.

**Agar**  There's a lot of farmers watching what you do.

**William**  Yer can't keep a secret farming. To find out what someone's up to all yer gorra do is look over the hedge.

**Agar**  If they look over your hedge they'll see a brand new car. A telephone.

**William**  If they tek up pig farming they'll need a system.

*AGAR fiddles with the pig info system.*

**Agar**  It's a little like playing God I imagine. What would He have written on your card?

**William**  That I'm the happiest man alive. What's He gorr on yourn?

**Agar**  That I complicate life.

71

**William**  Life's easy enough. Weddings on a Satdi, Births on a Mondi, funerals on a Fridi.

*WILLIAM pours more whisky.*

I've heard say yer don't gerr involved in the farm side of things on the estate ovver much these days. Driving down here for your muck every Thursday to stand in this kitchen is all the farming yer do.

**Agar**  She is the most compelling individual female I have ever met.

*Enter STEFAN.*

**Stefan**  Hello sir!

**Agar**  Guten tag.

**Stefan**  (*To AGAR.*) It's muck day is it?

(*To WILLIAM.*) Guess Will! Go on guess!

**William**  Thirteen?

**Stefan**  Fifteen!

**William**  (*In awe.*) Bloody hell.

**Stefan**  One of our sows has just had a litter of fifteen.

*Enter MAUDIE in a state of joy.*

**Maudie**  Fifteen! Will! Fifteen!

*MAUDIE goes to wash her hands at the kitchen sink.*

**William**  Aye, I've heard. Yer'd better write to Harold Macmillan.

**Maudie**  Oh! Hello sir! Dint see yer hiding there sir, sorry.

**Agar**  Good afternoon. Fifteen. What breed of boar?

**William**  Secret project.

*There is a cry from the bathroom.*

**Stefan**  Excuse me?!

*STEFAN exits to the bathroom.*

**Maudie**  God, that's all we need! That's our Laura, she had a show today. It must be all the excitement.

**William**  Pig farms are well known for their dangerous levels of excitement. We should have warning notices up.

**Maudie**  Yer daft in the head you. Excuse me sir.

*MAUDIE exits to the bathroom. WILLIAM goes to the pig information system and writes up Chloe's card. AGAR watches.*

**Agar**  This is a factory.

**William**  Part factory, part genetic laboratory, part gold-mine.

**Agar**  When do you stop? You don't have the labour to run two thousand pigs.

**William**  I'll hire a pigman. Pay wages.

**Agar**  Mixed farming, for these little family units was a good system, you know. Feed the cereals to the livestock, use the manure to feed the fields, to grow more cereals, to feed to the animals. A cycle. There was poetry in it. The rhythm of life in accord with the seasons.

**William**  It's 1958. The poor want meat.

**Agar**  Do they? Oh dear. They don't want meat every day do they?

**William**  Why should they eat any less well than you?

**Agar**  Let's not get political again William. I've got a sore throat.

*Enter MAUDIE in a rush.*

**Maudie**  She's bloody started! Phone the doctor, yer know I don't like using that thing. Sorry sir.

*WILLIAM goes over to the phone.*

**William**  Calm down, she's onny giving birth. Yer only at top pitch cos yer never had none yersen.

**Maudie**  You'll bloody pay for that William Harrison! Sorry sir.

**William**  Stop fucking 'sorry sir'-ing!

*Exit MAUDIE to bathroom.*

(*On the phone.*) Hello love… Aye, Doctor Wilson at Driffield… Ta…

*Enter MAUDIE.*

**Maudie**  Sorry sir, we need to lift her…

**Agar**  I see.

*AGAR exits to bathroom. MAUDIE stands by the phone stressing WILLIAM.*

**William**  (*On the phone.*) It's William Harrison here, Kilham Wold… Aye, oh not so bad ta, how are you love?…

**Maudie**  – gerr on with it!

**William**  – well I never… It's our Laura she's started… Aye… Well I don't know what was arranged burr if he don't come out sharpish he's gonna miss the fun by the sounds of it.

*Commotion as LAURA is carried in by AGAR and STEFAN.*

**Laura**  Put me down. I'm alright, I'll walk!

**William**  (*On phone.*) Can you hear that?… Aye, well that's all them going mad… Right you are. Tarra.

(*To MAUDIE.*) He's coming to the phone.

*They set LAURA down, she walks crab-like, with one hand on each knee, into the bedroom. AGAR and STEFAN follow, the door closes.*

**William**  (*Intense.*) Gerr him out that room.

*MAUDIE goes off. During the next AGAR enters.*

(*On the phone.*) …Hello Doctor Wilson… It's not me, no. Last time I had trouble wi' me legs Jesus was still looking for work as a carpenter… It's our Laura, she's a week early, but she's started… I wun't know if her waters had broken, hang on, I'll find out.

**Agar**  Yes. They have.

**William**  (*On the phone.*) Aye, they have… Kilham Wold Farm, past Driffield, yon side of Fimber… Yer know the Agar estate, aye, well yer pass them gates and then yer go about three mile and our post is there on yer left burr it's gorra sack over it for the ket man, so you're looking for a post with a bag over it, alright? How long'll yer be? … Righteo. Over and out.

*Phone down.*

Half hour. And he'll get lost as usual an'all.

**Agar**  What do you have for the ket man?

**William**  Dead sow.

**Agar**  I'll take it for the hounds.

**William**  I get money off the ket man.

**Agar**  I'll pay. I'll take it with the muck.

**William**  Two shilling.

*AGAR pays up. LAURA cries out off.*

The sow's on the rulley. Yon side of shed two.

*The squire doesn't move. Enter STEFAN.*

**Stefan**  (*To AGAR.*) Thanks for your help, sir.

(*To WILLIAM.*) What's happening?!

**William**  He's on his way.

**Stefan**  (*Panicking.*) Maudie's panicking Uncle Will!

**William**  Oh aye? And you're not?

*Cries from LAURA. Enter MAUDIE.*

**Stefan**  Sheisse!

**Maudie**  Steff! Come in here and hold her hand at least.

*Exit STEFAN.*

**Agar**  Should I do some hot water Mrs Harrison? And towels?

**Maudie**  Yer can if yer like but what the bloody hell I'm supposed to do with hot water and towels I do not know!

*AGAR goes to the sink and starts filling a kettle. WILLIAM pours a whisky.*

Oh Will! I've not gorr a good feeling about this one! What we need is someone who knows what they're bloody doing.

**William**  He's set off. Yer've midwifed fifteen already today, so –

**Maudie**  – he's the wrong way round or summat! I'm at top pitch!

*MAUDIE snaffles the whisky and leaves to go back into the bedroom. During the next there are further cries.*

**William**  (*To AGAR.*) Go. The sow is on the rulley.

*Big cry from LAURA.*

**Agar**  I love her.

**William**  Yer don't know what love is. The real thing's a lot more fun but a lot more complicated than that med up stuff of yourn.

*Cries off. Louder, desperate.*

**Agar**  William! I think I can help in there! I may not know anything about love but I do know about childbirth!

**William**  Yer 'separated' siamese twins on an ice flo with a cake knife and a bottle of rum.

**Agar**  I researched that chapter thoroughly! I went to Barts in London! My friend was a doctor!

**William**  Both them siamese twins died.

**Agar**  In the book! I can help in there, I know I can!

*Cries off. Desperate. STEFAN comes out.*

**Stefan**  Oh God, what are we gonna do Will?! The baby's stuck. I think he's the wrong way round.

**William**  We can all help her, by keeping calm.

**Stefan**  Does the doctor know where he's coming?

**Agar**  (*To STEFAN.*) I have no medical training as such Mr Harrison, but I had to research childbirth very thoroughly for my book. My very best friend was a doctor. Have you read the book?

**Stefan**  'Cannibal!'? Yes. I've read it. What – !

**Agar**  – The birth of the siamese twins?

**William**  They both died!

**Stefan**  What's this – [about?]

**Agar**  – In the book, yes!

**Stefan**  Can someone – [explain to me what you're talking about.]

**William**  – I've tawld the squire to go!

**Agar**  I can save Laura! Don't you see I can save her.

*AGAR starts to move towards the bedroom.*

**William**  Stop him!

**Stefan**  (*Grabbing him.*) Sir! Please!

**William**  I'm norr 'aving you seeing that girl!

*The cry of a newborn child silences them. STEFAN goes in.*

She int the only woman in the world yer know. Yer family's gorr a big house in London, so tek yersen down there. What yer need is a concentration of women of yer own sort. Yer not gonna get that round here. I know all you big families talk to each other, but obviously they an't come up with owt suitable for you. It's London yer wanna be. (*Beat.*) So we're done. There'll be a new load of muck next Thursday. And yer'll find out then if this un's a boy or girl.

*Exit AGAR. More baby crying. Enter STEFAN with a big grin on his face.*

What we got this time?

*To black.*

# 1979

## *A Roman Road*

*1979. Summer. Morning, about ten o'clock. The pig information system is still there. There is an array of white goods, and other signs of modernisation. Fluorescent lighting replaces bulbs. Four framed photos of four girls on separate graduation days hang on the walls. The sound of 'What Do I Get?' by The Buzzcocks is heard from behind a closed bedroom door. That bedroom door opens and ALAN enters. He is 22 and dressed in pyjama bottoms and a black Ramones T-shirt. He turns the kettle on and pours himself a bowl of cornflakes with milk and lots of sugar. He starts eating them, as he goes back to his bedroom. Once in the bedroom he turns the music up, and closes the door. Enter TITCH. He is about 30. A huge man. He wears denims and has a jeans jacket tied by the arms around his waist. His chest is covered by a red singlet with the logo of Status Quo. His hair is farmer's boy long in the cut of the day. He carries a small buff card.*

**Titch** 'ello!

*He looks at the buff card in his hand.*

Mr Hohen…Hohenstauf…fuck! HELLO!

*He sits at the table which is set as it normally is, i.e. running lengthways from stage left to stage right. He lights a cigarette. He seems confused and annoyed by the positioning of the table. After some thought he picks up the table and, in one movement, turns it through ninety degrees so it is running upstage to downstage. ALAN enters from upstairs.*

How do!?

**Alan** You've moved the table.

**Titch**  Aye! Felt all wrong! You a student? Student music. What yer studying?

**Alan**  Psychology.

**Titch**  Yer gonna be a psychiatrist then?

**Alan**  Psychology is the study of normal behaviour.

**Titch**  What's that then?

**Alan**  What do you want?

**Titch**  Come for the job. Where's yer dad?

**Alan**  I'll get him.

*ALAN exits to the fold yard. TITCH sits and smokes. Enter LAURA from the bathroom. She jumps, seeing TITCH.*

**Laura**  Agh! Yer give me the fright of me life!

**Titch**  Come for the interview.

**Laura**  Who moved the table?

**Titch**  Me. I tawld the punk.

**Laura**  You moved the table?

**Titch**  Aye, it dun't mek any sense running east to west.

**Laura**  We don't have any jobs, I think –

**Titch**  What's this then?!

*LAURA takes the card from TITCH but doesn't read it. Enter STEFAN, ALAN and Uncle WILLIAM.*

Eh up! Here we go!

**Laura**  We an't gorr any jobs have we?

**Stefan**  I put a card in the job centre for a pigman.

**Laura**  We don't need a pigman.

*TITCH stands, as if to go.*

**Titch**  Are yer watching?! That's me! I'm off! I've come all the way from Beeford. It's a fair distance you know. Yer wun't wanna be dragged by yer balls from here to Beeford!

**Stefan**  Please, sit down. There is a job. I'm Stefan.

**Titch**  Steve Bolsover. Titch.

**Stefan**  This is Will.

**Titch**  Alright Will! Got no legs?

**William**  I'm an amputee.

**Titch**  Above the knee or below the knee? Don't tell me. I don't wanna know. Gives me the willies.

**Laura**  Can someone tell me why I've not been told that we're advertising for staff?

**Stefan**  Look love, I'm sorry but –

**Laura**  (*To WILLIAM.*) – Do you know about this?

**William**  Aye.

**Stefan**  Laura!

**Laura**  I don't know why I bother.

**Stefan**  – Laura! Please.

*LAURA exits in a huff.*

**Titch**  Glad she's gone. All men together now. Swear, talk bollocks. Do what the fuck we like, eh!?

**William**  Who moved the table?

**Titch**  Look! I'm gerrin fucking sick of this table business! I did. If I don't get the job yer can move it back to where it were afore.

*ALAN exits upstairs.*

He's had enough. Is this an interview then?

**Stefan**  It's not unfair for us to want a know a little more about you is it?

**Titch**  I'm me. Titch. That's it. You had anyone else for this job?

**Stefan**  Not yet.

**Titch**  That's it then innit.

**William**  Where do you live?

**Titch**  I'm not tellin' yer.

**William**  Where did you sleep last night?

**Titch**  In me car.

**Stefan**  Okay. So you've got a full driving licence?

**Titch**  Course I fucking have.

**William**  What was your last job?

**Titch**  Benson's.

**Stefan**  I half know Daniel. He's a wonderful character isn't he, and –

**Titch**  – He's a bastard. If I ever see the fucker again I'll kill him.

**William**  Why did you leave?

**Titch**  Sacked us.

**Stefan**  And why exactly did he dismiss you?

**Titch**  He caught me nicking stuff.

**William**  What were yer stealing?

**Titch**  Red diesel.

**William**  Do you have any of the relevant City and Guilds
stockman qualifications?

**Titch**  Fuck off! I like pigs.

**Stefan**  What exactly is it that you like about working with
pigs?

**Titch**  They're intelligent animals. They're clever but not
that clever. Just enough to mek it interesting but not
enough to get yer worried.

**Stefan**  Are you married?

**Titch**  No woman's ever gonna get the better of me.

**Stefan**  You're not married then?

**Titch**  Look, if I need a fuck I know where to go, alright?!

**William**  How many sows has Benson got now?

**Titch**  He's running about three hundred Large Whites.
He's got three big fuck off Warcup sheds, concrete floors,
automatic feeding, ventilation. It's like the last scene
in a James Bond film, you know, big shed of a place
with everyone running about and pressing buttons. It's
like that but without the bikinis. Onny problem with
Benson's place is him. He's a total and complete fucking
cunt.

**Stefan**  He's in a scheme with Tesco's, yeah?

**Titch**  Aye, they've gorr him by the balls.

**William**  How long does he take to gerr 'em to bacon
weight?

**Titch**  Six month by rights. What about you?

**Stefan**  We're working towards that.

**Titch**  I bet. One look at them sheds of yourn and I could
tell yer was amateurs. I bet yer've got one clapped out

auld boar who can't gerr it up unless you whack him on the arse with a shovel.

**Stefan** Actually, we have seven Norwegian Landrace boars. We collect ourselves and distribute using deep catheterisation.

**Titch** (*Stands and shakes hands with them both.*) Worr I'm doing now, is apologising. I was obviously fucking way off. Alright. I've sat down again now. I'm impressed.

**William** Stefan went on a course at Bishop Burton college.

**Titch** Oh aye. I'm banned from there.

**Stefan** What for?

**Titch** Dunno, forgotten. Apparently, I've repressed it. How d'yer catch the sperm? Yer got a saddle?

**Stefan** Yes. We've had a few disasters but I've got them trained now.

**Titch** Have you ever had a go on it yersen? The saddle?

Go on! You have an't yer! Course you have! Had a little go on there when no-one's looking. Ha, ha! I have. Live fast die young me! I'm worried about them sheds though. They look fucked to me.

*Enter LAURA. She messes about in the sink area aggressively, and then leaves.*

Yer not gonna get rocked to sleep tonight pal!

**Stefan** My wife and I, and Uncle Will of course, we make all the decisions as a family, but this is a little delicate, er… I'm not well and er…actually it's quite a serious condition and –

**Titch** – don't tell me! Yer not well and you an't tawld her!? What yer got?

**Stefan** It's not unrelated to emphysema and –

**Titch**  – Pal of mine had that, wheezing and coughing he
wor, and he went to the doctor and doctor said it wor
emphysema and BANG – three month later he were
dead!

**William**  I bought the sheds off the M.O.D. They were
good sheds, but needed lining.

**Titch**  A cawld pig is a thin pig.

**William**  I chose asbestos. Stef lined each one of them three
sheds hissen.

**Titch**  On yer tod?

**Stefan**  Yes.

**William**  Cutting, sawing, shaving.

**Titch**  (*To STEFAN.*) Do you blame him then? Has that
come between yer? I mean, it in't murder, obviously, he
din't mean it did he. Now he's blaming hissen. How do
you feel about that? Him blaming hissen?

**Stefan**  No-one knew about asbestos then. Going back to
Benson's, what's his feed situation? He's got no land that
I know of.

**Titch**  They're not his pigs you know. Fimber Feed own the
pigs, Benson's just finishing 'em for him. They're the best
Fimber Feed. They turn up once a month blow it into
the bins and fuck off. What do you do for feed here?

**Stefan**  We grow some of our own, mix it ourselves. For
historical reasons, didn't want to get involved with
Fimber Feed. Can you plough?

**Titch**  (*Standing.*) I'm a specialist pig man. I'm not
ploughing fields, and bloody harvesting, and pratting
about mixing up feed. Yer'll have me fucking Morris
Dancing next!

*TITCH makes to go.*

Are yer watching this!? I'm off!

**Stefan**  Mr Bolsover!

**William**  Titch! Please 'ang on.

**Stefan**  We're gonna rationalise down to four acres!

**William**  We've decided to sell the arable!

**Titch**  What's stopping yer then?

**Stefan**  It's a family farm.

**Titch**  Oh I gerrit. It's her is it?

**Stefan**  Laura hasn't yet understood the implications of my illness.

*TITCH sits down.*

**Titch**  Did you see that? I was up and off, but now I'm sat down again. Burr I'm not ploughing! It bores the tits off me. Look – it's obvious what yer have to do here. Get shot of the arable, buy some Warcup sheds, and get yersen a contract with Fimber Feed. Do that, and I'm yours.

**Stefan**  It's not that easy to sell one's inheritance.

**Titch**  I'll tell yer summat for nowt, that punk son of yours in't gonna be farming this land after you've jumped the stick.

**Stefan**  I'm very proud of my son. He's doing a PhD in Educational Psychology.

**Titch**  Like I said, neither use nor ornament. Meks yer sick I bet, eh? Yer build summat up like this, pay for him through school, they fill his head with shit, and then you end up with no-one to pass yer business on to. Is he yer onny son?

**Stefan**  Yes. I have four daughters.

**Titch**  Oh aye?

**Stefan**  They're all married.

**Titch**  You're not facing up to realities here are yer. You're dying, you got no legs AND you're not a spring chicken, and milado up there's off with fairies. All yer gorr is me. In a few years time it'll be just me and her.

*Pause. Silence. STEFAN puts his head in his hands. He takes some time to recover.*

Have I upset yer? Sorry. But that's me, that's Titch Bolsover, I'm straight, I'm a fucking Roman Road.

*Pause. STEFAN recovers.*

**Stefan**  Okay.

**Titch**  I wanna live in, but listen, I'm not working Sundays.

**Stefan**  Ah! You're a Christian?

**Titch**  No. I've gorr a drink problem. I get very badly pissed most Satdi nights. I want me own room, double bed, teasmaid. I'm not sleeping on a couple bags of chaff in the barn like a fucking Paddy. I'm not interested in the money. It's living in I want. A fried breakfast, cooked dinner, and a decent tea. I'm not eating margarine. I work hard I want butter.

**Stefan**  I'll need to discuss this with my wife.

**Titch**  Aye you do that. I'll go have a look round and come back in ten minutes.

**Stefan**  She might say no. We run the farm, er… collectively. Discuss everything.

**Titch**  Cept you an't told her yer dying.

*TITCH leaves. STEFAN puts his head back in his hands.*

**William**  Y'alright son?

**Stefan**  Yes, thank you. What do you think of him?

**William**  He's bloody perfect.

**Stefan**  Yes. It's a kind of miracle.

*Enter LAURA with two or three pig catheters. She starts to wash them at the sink and then pegs them up to dry.*

**Laura**  – yer interviewing men to work on my farm and I don't know owt about it!

*Enter ALAN from upstairs with a coffee mug.*

**Stefan**  We need to talk.

**Laura**  Bloody right we need to talk!

*ALAN puts the coffee mug in the sink and goes to get a clean mug from the cupboard.*

Use the same mug! What do you think this is an hotel?

**Alan**  Don't take it out on me!

**Laura**  Don't put owt in there when these is dripping.

**Alan**  Oh fuck!

**Laura**  Don't swear in this house! You can leave your Surrey talk in Surrey.

**Alan**  You're drying artificial insemination equipment over the kitchen sink.

**Laura**  They're clean!

**Alan**  This is disgusting.

**Laura**  Aye, owt to do wi' work's disgusting to you.

**Alan**  Do you want a coffee Uncle Will? Dad.

**William**  No ta. Yer dad dun't want owt.

*ALAN looks at his dad, head in hands. He searches in cupboards for biscuits.*

**Alan**  We got any biscuits?

**Laura**  Second cupboard.

**William**  We need new buildings Laura. We need to sell the arable.

**Laura**  That's an old idea, and a bad'n an'all. Four acres in't a farm.

**Stefan**  That's all we need.

**Laura**  Thirty year back, I came to this farm of me own free will. I wun't have come here if it were a four acre pig unit. I don't ever wanna be in a situation where if I tek a walk round Spittle Garth meadow I'm trespassing. Yer brother died for that field. Maudie – last thing she done before she took to her bed was walk the circuit down there.

**William**  Some of the best moments of my life have happened in that field.

**Laura**  (*Laughing.*) Don't embarrass me.

**Alan**  I think it's a good idea.

**Laura**  Shurrup you. If you had any interest in this place then yer can have a say, but you ain't, you never had, so put a biscuit in it.

(*To WILLIAM.*) Sell the land and we're dependent on the feed companies.

**William**  We're gerrin twenty quid a pig Laura, the margins are alright.

**Laura**  I know. I like me foreign holidays, I like me new cars, I like the fact that every single one of my daughters has upped and offed to university and become so bloody full of themselves that I never see them.

**William**  We an't got the labour to run eighty acres.

**Laura**  Stef manages. Don't yer? What's up? The doctor said it were nowt. Yer've bin mekking the most of that cough for the best part of ten years. Anyone would think you were on yer last legs.

**Alan**  These biscuits have gone soft. Where are the chocolate digestives?

**Laura**  I've buried 'em. Up on the tops. It's a three mile walk uphill and then you've gorra dig 'em out the hole. With a bit of luck it'll be raining. There's spades out the back. Why don't you tek The Ramones up there with you, they look like they could do with the exercise.

**Alan**  Tut! I'm outa here.

*ALAN goes off up the stairs.*

**Stefan**  I need to talk to you.

**William**  I'll be in me barn then. If yer need me.

*WILLIAM exits.*

**Laura**  All I'm saying is every morning I'm up at six, I cook you breakfast, and then I'm straight in the farrowing house. The least I expect from you two is an equal say –

**Stefan**  – Laura!

**Laura**  Having a cough is no excuse for becoming ignorant! There's no way we're selling the arable. Over my dead body.

*STEFAN stands and goes to the foot of the stairs.*

**Stefan**  Alan!

**Laura**  What's gooin on?

**Stefan** ALAN!!

*ALAN opens his bedroom door. The sound of Joy Division's 'New Dawn Fades' is heard.*

**Alan** What?

**Stefan** Come down here, I want to talk to you.

**Alan** What is it now?!

**Stefan** Just come down here!

**Alan** (*Quietly.*) Oh fucking hell.

**Laura** What is it Stef? Tell me! What's gooin on?

*ALAN comes down the stairs and stands stock still. STEFAN can't find the words and his bottom lip starts puckering. LAURA softens and takes him in her arms. They hold each other to the sound of 'New Dawn Fades'. ALAN just stands there looking at the floor. Enter TITCH. He stands and watches, and actually manages to be unobtrusive.*

*To black.*

# 1995
# Suffragette

*1995. Autumn. Early afternoon. A CD player. A computer on a workstation stand with printer. A modern telephone and fax. The pig information system has gone. WILLIAM is not using the computer but is in a modern motorised wheelchair. A streamer on the wall declares: '100 NOT OUT!!'. WILLIAM is blowing up balloons, painstakingly slowly. LAURA enters in coat, with shopping.*

**Laura** Foggy.

**William**  We better call it off then. Did yer gerr a balloon pump?

**Laura**  Bugger. I knew I'd forgotten something. I hope I've gorr enough food here. How many have you invited?

**William**  There's a small village outside Mexico City called Quarrapas, population of about three hundred. They're all coming.

**Laura**  Yer get worse you. Have yer heard?

**William**  Aye. Went peacefully, unfortunately.

**Laura**  Now, now, come on. His son's come up from London. Teken ovver.

**William**  What's he called?

**Laura**  The same I think.

**William**  Poor bugger. Finding out that yer dad's called Primrose must be bad enough but not as bad as discovering that you are an'all.

*Enter a young woman VET, about 26, a Kiwi. She knocks on the door even though it's open.*

**Laura**  Yer done love?

**Vet**  I need to fill out the scheme form, yeah.

**Laura**  Here, sit at the table. There's tea in the pot.

**Vet**  Thanks.

*VET sits at the table. And starts completing some paperwork. LAURA pours her a tea.*

Is he alright yeah. Your pigman?

**Laura**  Titch? What did he do?

**Vet**  He just seemed to get rarked up real easy, yeah?

**William**  He doesn't like women.

**Laura**  Three reasons he wouldn't warm to you. One – yer a young lass and he thinks yer don't know what yer talking about. Two – yer a foreigner. And three – yer educated.

**William**  And on top of all that –  he's dead ignorant.

**Vet**  You're quite incredible for a hundred Mr Harrison.

**William**  Ta. Are yer courtin' love?

**Vet**  (*Laughs.*) No.

**William**  D'yer like ten pin bowling?

**Laura**  Shurrup will yer! She might not like older men.

**William**  I'm not auld. I just bin here longer.

**Vet**  What do you feel about a young Kiwi 'lass' telling you what you can and can't do, yeah?

**Laura**  We'd do owt that supermarket asked us to do to get that susstification stamp. Me, I'd cut me right hand off. What would you do Uncle Will?

**William**  I'd streak naked through Woolworths. Again. If yer don't stamp us she'll have to go work in the Little Chef.

*Silence. The VET gets back to filling in her form, rather self-consciously since LAURA and WILLIAM do nothing but watch her.*

**Vet**  I didn't get a sense, yeah, that Titch knew what the broken needles protocol was, is, yeah?

*LAURA stands and goes looking for a file on the shelf.*

Did you get a telegram from the Queen, yeah?

**William**  About broken needles? No. She's not that keen on pigs. She's more horses.

**Laura**  Behave!

(*Passing a file over.*) That's the needles book. It in't a telegram no more. It's a letter.

*LAURA shows her the letter. She looks at it, the envelope etc.*

**Vet**  Wow. Thank you. Fantastic. Do you have any tips on longevity?

**William**  Get yer legs chopped off when you're twennie-one. Are them sheds alright?

*She hands it back to LAURA. She goes back to the form.*

**Vet**  They're excellent buildings.

**William**  Ta.

**Vet**  Can I see your feed delivery records, yeah?

*LAURA goes to get another file.*

How much credit do you have with Fimber Feed?

**Laura**  What right has that supermarket got to ask about my finances?

**Vet**  It's a question on the form, I'm sorry, yeah.

**William**  We got three months credit with 'em.

**Vet**  (*Writing.*) And your feed bill is thirty-three thousand pounds a month. So you owe them ninety-nine thousand pounds, yeah?

**William**  It's ovver an 'undred as it happens. It got to an hundred afore I did.

**Vet**  Aren't they worried about that?

**William**  It's exactly what they want.

**Laura**  They've gorr us right where they want us. The squire in't gonna be worried about a hundred thousand pounds when Brussels chucks two million quid a year his way – money he don't even need.

**Vet**  I beg your pardon, who's the squire?

**Laura**  Fimber Feed.

**Vet**  Right. Yeah, you'd be in a better position if you could grow your own feed.

**Laura**  (*Looks at WILLIAM.*) D'yer hear that?

**Vet**  (*Incredulous.*) Why do you do this? Pig farming?

**William**  It's a good laugh. (*Laughs.*) When one of them gets out! Kaw!

**Laura**  D'yer remember when that gilt escaped and ran down the main road?

**William**  (*Laughing.*) Aye. 1976 that hot summer! Aye, that's me favourite!

**Laura**  (*Laughing.*) Ran half way to Driffield!

**Vet**  You're losing fifty pounds for every finished pig. I just don't see why you do it, yeah?

**William**  We can't all be conceptual artists – there'd be nowt to eat.

**Laura**  It's not what we do. It's what we are. We're farmers.

**William**  That's not her talking there. That's summat someone said in the Guardian.

**Vet**  I can't give you the accreditation stamp.

*Pause.*

You're using stalls for the dry sows. That's illegal – now, yeah.

**Laura**  You tek the backs off them stalls and I'll guarantee yer, they don't go nowhere. We got 'em trained to it. All our pigs is happy pigs, in't they Uncle Will.

**William**  Aye. Yer didn't mention this to Titch did yer?

**Vet**  I'm not saying they're suffering. They look fine to me but what I'm saying is, you're still using stalls, yeah, and the date has gone, yeah. Stalls are illegal in the UK.

**Laura**  We're in the European Community. Stalls aren't illegal in Europe.

**William**  (*To LAURA.*) Leave her be Laura! It in't her doing.

(*To the VET.*) Sorry love, she's got all political.

**Vet**  This is British law. Your government – [they've chosen to…]

**Laura**  – We went to Blackpool yesterday!

*The VET is puzzled and looks to WILLIAM for clarification.*

**William**  Aye, we did.

**Vet**  We were talking about the Animal Welfare legislation, yeah, and then you tell me that you went to Blackpool yesterday.

**Laura**  To see the minister.

**William**  A lot of us in a bus.

**Laura**  The government want us all to go out of business!

**William**  She's been hell to live with ever since she went and got hersen politicised.

**Laura**  You had your war, I've got mine!

**William**  There's ovver much meat out there!

**Laura**  We're gonna picket Hull docks tomorrow –

**William**  – I'm not gooin! I'm having a lie-in!

**Laura**  – You're coming with us!

**William**  – I'm an 'undred fucking years auld and I'll have a fucking lie-in whenever I fucking want!

**Laura**  (*To VET.*) There's forty thousand carcasses come in every week through them docks –

**William**  – Leave her alone. Yer embarrassing!

**Vet**  We inspect those carcasses. They're Dutch. It's all legal.

**Laura**  – Dutch my arse. They're onny butchered in Holland.

**William**  It's not her fault!

**Laura**  Mark my words, all them Polish, or Yugoslavian pigs'll be tethered.

**William**  She's come from the other side of the bloody world and she's going round Europe in a camper van tomorrow. So give her a break.

**Laura**  Yer not gonna stamp us are yer?

**Vet**  How can I stamp you, yeah?

**William**  We're illegal! All of a sudden.

**Vet**  If you remove the stalls, and convert to loose housing, I'm sure you'll be considered for the scheme in the future. The sheds are in good condition. You could run this place as a finishing unit for a feed company. I know Fimber Feed do –

**Laura**  – I'm not working wage labour raising pigs for the bloody squire. Any pigs on this farm are gonna be

Harrison pigs! I've never had a penny in grants from
Europe and yet him up the road with forty thousand
fucking acres gets two million quid a year he dunt need.

*Enter TITCH quickly. He is carrying a rope made into a noose.
He climbs up on to the table and puts the rope round a hook
and the noose round his neck. The vet stands and backs off.*

Titch? Titch!?

**William**  What yer doing?

**Titch**  Killin' mesen.

**Vet**  Oh my God!

**William**  Don't worry love, he's all mouth and no trousers.

**Titch**  That lass there, she's insulted me.

**Laura**  What's she said?

**Titch**  She ses I'm mistreating my girls.

**Vet**  I never said that.

**Titch**  You tek the backs off them stalls, and none of 'em'll
go nowhere. I've never used tethering. None of my
fucking girls have ever been tethered.

(*To LAURA.*) Have yer got me dinner?

*LAURA takes his dinner out the oven and passes it up to
him. He eats as he talks.*

**Vet**  I've recorded that. The sows are no longer tethered.

**Titch**  I've never had 'em tethered.

**Laura**  Aye, that's true. We've never tethered 'em.

**Vet**  Alright, I'll put something in the margin, yeah?

*She writes.*

**Titch** You've hurt me feelings. Look at me! Is this normal behaviour?

**Laura** Don't kill yersen Titch.

**William** It's yer pub quiz tomorrow.

**Titch** Don't try psychology on me. It's never worked, never will.

(*Of the meal, to LAURA.*) This is good this Laura, ta.

**Laura** Thanks Titch.

**William** Who's yer pub quiz match agin?

**Titch** Old White Hart. Them fucking bastard cheating paraplegics.

**Laura** Come down Titch love.

**Titch** No. I'm a suffragette.

**William** Yer can't kill yersen until yer've fixed me up a string to the fuse-box in the porch. Like yer promised.

*TITCH looks to the porch.*

**Laura** Yer've forgotten about that an't yer?

**Titch** Sorry I'll do it... Look! She int gonna stamp us is she?

**Laura** We'll borrow the money off the bank and convert to loose housing.

**William** Yer can play football with 'em then.

**Titch** Aye?

**William** Aye.

**Titch** No. I'm gonna kill mesen. (*Pointing at the VET.*) Cos of you!

**Laura** We love yer Titch.

**Titch**  Who fucking does?

**Laura**  Everyone. Yer brilliant. Yer light up our lives.

**Titch**  I din't set out to try an' light up anyone's life. I'm just fucking me.

**Laura**  That's what we like. You. Yer great.

**William**  Yer lovable.

**Titch**  I'm not fucking lovable, I'm fucking upset!

**Laura**  We can see yer upset.

**William**  She's onny doing her job.

**Titch**  My girls are happy! If you tek the backs off them stalls –

**Vet**  – I know. They won't go 'nowhere', yeah?

**William**  She can't stamp us. We're illegal.

**Titch**  What we gonna do then?

**William**  Yer could retrain as a computer game designer.

**Laura**  Shurrup! It's no laughing matter – he's gonna kill hissen.

**William**  He 'eckers like gonna kill hissen!

**Titch**  I will. I'm gonna jump now! Here tek me plate.

*The VET runs out.*

**William**  Yer an't gorr an audience now.

**Laura**  Come down Titch love. I'll put yer favourite record on. I'll dance with yer.

*LAURA goes to the CD player and puts on Dr. Hook's 'When You're In Love With A Beautiful Woman'. TITCH slips his head out the noose.*

**Titch**  Dint wanna upset her. People can tek things the wrong way, eh?

*Dr Hook's 'When You're In Love With a Beautiful Woman' plays. He dances close with LAURA.*

This song's fucking brilliant Uncle Will. Listen to the lyrics.

*He sings along to the song, repeating lyrics for the benefit of WILLIAM.*

Are yer having a good birthday Will?!

**William**  Aye. Ta.

**Laura**  Happy?

**William**  I'm happy that Maudie never saw this day.

**Titch**  Count yer blessings!

**William**  I got me health. You two have gorr each other.

*TITCH and LAURA dance.*

*Lights fade to black.*

# 2005
# A Song In Your Heart

*2005. A January evening. It's dark. Some of the windows are broken; some are boarded up. Ivy and weeds are growing freely on the outside of the house and some ivy has crept in through a window. The table has gone. On the floor are lots of plastic ready-meal containers, unopened post, and Tesco plastic carrier bags. The carrier bags are sellotaped to the windows. On the floor is a single mattress. The TV has a lottery ticket sellotaped to the screen. The room is in darkness.*

*A loop tape plays in a ghetto blaster on the work top. It is a 'security tape'. That is, it is the sound of a dog barking, then the sound of a hoover hoovering, then the sound of a drill, then the sound of someone mixing a gin and tonic with ice, then a toilet flushing, then back to a dog barking and then repeat for at least three cycles. The sound of breaking glass off stage left in the bathroom area. Enter DANNY, a young man of about 25. He turns the light on.*

**Danny**  (*Shouted.*) 's only me!! (*Laughs.*)

*He turns the tape off. He takes the tape out and looks at it. DANNY goes over to the gun cabinet and tries the door. It's locked. Enter BLUE.*

Filth in here! Farmers eh? They're fucking animals.

*DANNY gives BLUE the tape.*

It were a tape.

**Blue**  Innovations Report. Told you.

*BLUE tries the door of the gun cabinet. He then runs his hand along the top of the kitchen cabinets looking for a key. DANNY finds a bottle of whisky and pours two very generous glasses. BLUE pulls out a drawer from the kitchen cabinet puts it on the floor, in the light, and starts sifting through it. DANNY does the same with a second drawer.*

I got caught by a Securignome once in Goole.

**Danny**  A what?

**Blue**  A Securignome. It's a garden gnome fitted with an optical PIR body heat resonance indicator.

**Danny**  You were nicked by a fucking garden gnome?

**Blue**  I didn't say I was proud of it. One of the seven dwarfs. Dopey.

*DANNY slugs his whisky down and goes for a top-up. BLUE watches him.*

I'm driving back. You were driving at eighty-five miles an hour in a thirty limit.

**Danny**  I was thinking about sex. You know that massage parlour down Humber Street, top of the old fruit market?

**Blue**  I've never been.

**Danny**  They got this big Chinese tart there, bowt twennie stone. Smells like a fucking horse what has been eating Chinese food. Always got a dirty arse. I love it. Why do I like that?

**Blue**  Cos you're mentally ill.

**Danny**  What are we looking for?

**Blue**  The key to the gun cabinet.

**Danny**  No keys in there. I couldn't live out here.

*DANNY puts the drawer back and inspects the kitchen. He finds a laundry bag in a draw and sets it in the middle of the room and fills it with anything he finds he likes, which is very little.*

**Blue**  If I won the lottery I might get mesen a big house in the country. Little beef herd. They look beautiful cattle. Hobby farming they call it. My Auntie had a dairy farm near Hornsea. But it fell into the sea. Do you know how much a bacon sarnie should cost?

**Danny**  What do you mean should cost?

**Blue**  If the farmer over the last hundred years had not scientifically bred the perfect bacon pig a bacon sandwich would cost about twenty-seven quid.

**Danny**  You're having a laugh.

**Blue**  Ignorant bastards though, people like you, when you're eating your two-fifty bacon butty, do you ever say, 'Thank God for the genius of the British farmer, he's just saved me twenty-four pound fifty'? No, you say, 'Fucking hell! – two pound fifty for a poxy bacon sarnie, that's a bit of an ask!'

**Danny**  Yeah, yeah.

**Blue**  They don't have to do it. They could get out of bed one morning and say, 'Fuck this for a game of soldiers, I think I'll sign on and do a bit of nicking.' We don't appreciate the farmer in this country. Why? Cos we've always had the empire. In France 'peasant' is a term of fucking endearment. Why? Cos – the French respect the farmer, and the mad thing is compared to our farmers the French are fucking useless. Three cows, two chickens and one fucking duck – and that is a BIG French farm.

**Danny**  I like to listen to you talking. It's all that stuff you read in't it.

**Blue**  It's not just the reading. It's an orientation innit.

**Danny**  Yeah. You could stand for Parliament, Blue, go on, why don't yer?

**Blue**  Cos I'm a burglar.

**Danny**  So?

(*Beat.*) It's about time we had some representation in Parliament. There's a lot of Paki MPs.

**Blue**  You need to get out of the city more. Gerr a bit of air in yer lungs. Bit of green. Gerr a garden.

**Danny**  I'm never having another garden! Gardening – it's a fucking minefield!

**Blue**  Key!

*BLUE produces a small key. Walks over to the gun cabinet and tries the lock. It doesn't fit.*

I believe that is the key to an electric socket safe. Do the sockets. Here.

*BLUE hands DANNY a screwdriver. DANNY starts on the sockets. The phone rings. The answerphone kicks in. It is LAURA's voice. They light up ciggies.*

**Laura**  (*On answerphone.*) This is the answerphone for Mrs Laura Harrison. I might not be in. But I might be in but not answering the phone. If you're a burglar I've gorr a gun. (*Laugh.*) Thank you very much for your call.

*Beep.*

**Alan**  (*On the phone.*) Change that message mam. Happy birthday. Ring back, but don't forget that we're five hours behind. If you get Rebecca don't just put the phone down, she is my wife. She's sorry about what she said, but she's very passionate about the whole vegan thing. The kids have gone upstate for the weekend so don't ring back, unless you want to talk to me. Hope you had a good day.

*Beep.*

**Blue**  What did you learn from that message?

**Danny**  Er…Rebecca's a vegetarian.

**Blue**  Training you up is like tryna nail jelly to the ceiling. The woman here, lives alone.

**Danny**  How d'yer make that out?

**Blue**  'This is the answering service for Mrs Laura Harrison.' Not, 'You're through to Ben, Camilla, and Jasper,' like when you're doing a Kirkella house.

**Danny**  Here we go!

*DANNY has found a double socket behind which is a small safe. BLUE gives the key to DANNY and DANNY opens the safe. He tips the money on the floor.*

Wedding ring. It's a couple of quid. It's a pint.

*DANNY gives the ring to BLUE. DANNY picks up three first world war medals.*

**Blue**   First world war. Kenny'll have them.

**Danny**   What they worth?

**Blue**   Nowt much. What's that?

*He takes out an envelope and opens it.*

**Danny**   (*Reading.*) 'Her majesty is much interested to hear that you are celebrating your one hundredth birthday bla, bla, bla.' Picture of the Queen. Cheer up love it might never happen. William Harrison.

**Blue**   No key.

**Danny**   The old bird must be walking about with it.

**Blue**   Put the safe back.

**Danny**   In a minute. I need a shit.

**Blue**   Not in there.

**Danny**   Bit of a laugh. Shit in there. Screw it back in the wall. It's funny, what's the matter with yer?

**Blue**   You disgust me.

*DANNY squats and shits into the safe. BLUE takes his mobile out and dials a preset number.*

(*On the phone.*) Yeah, alright? ... Working hard... 1917 military medal, two bars... No?... Really? Fucking hell, an hero then?... The good news for us is he's dead, he was hundred years old in nineteen ninety-five... Would your American wannit?… I'll see you Monday after you've been to the bank then… Tarra Kenny.

*DANNY shows BLUE the results of his squat.*

You are fucking sick in the 'ead.

**Danny**  I get tense.

*During the next DANNY laughs as he puts the safe back and screws it back into the wall.*

**Blue**  Shh!! Car!

**Danny**  Fuck!

**Blue**  Kill the light! Get rid of that whisky! Get upstairs!

*BLUE and DANNY go up the stairs. Enter LAURA, now 85, and Mr LEWIS, a country solicitor of about 55. LAURA looks in a poor state, like a bag lady. She takes her coat off revealing a Little Chef waitress uniform.*

**Lewis**  Little Chef eh? The top. I like it.

**Laura**  Aye. I like it an'all. It's wipe clean.

**Lewis**  You don't still work there surely?

**Laura**  Oh no, I got too auld in the end. But they let me keep the top cos there's a burn on the sleeve. So we just wait for him then yeah?

**Lewis**  Yes. He said he'd be here at about half past seven.

**Laura**  He's late. I wanna sell him the house. I'm not having him just buying the sheds. I don't feel safe out here no more. There's onny one copper from here to Brid. And he can't find us. Turns up two weeks after I've rung, to see if I'm alright. I coulda been killed in them two weeks.

**Lewis**  Ah, now, my latest idea is rather an excellent one. Keep a telephone upstairs and if you have intruders downstairs then ring the police straight away and THEN order as many pizzas from as many different pizza restaurants as you can, because then within forty minutes or so you will have seven or eight young men on motorbikes all turning up at roughly the same time.

**Laura**  Am I allowed to shoot someone who comes on my land?

**Lewis**  Not if he's the postman. The postman is deemed to have a *presumed licence* to enter your unbuilt-upon private property. A meter reader also has a similar *presumed licence* to enter both your unbuilt-upon private property *and* your built-upon private property, however, if an individual who *prima facie* has such a presumed licence, whilst on your private property fosters a *larcenous* or *felonious* intent then his intention is related back by the *fiction of the law* so that he or she was deemed to be a trespasser from the moment he entered your property even though he was a meter reader when he or she – let's be fair – first did so. I know it sounds complicated Mrs Harrison but in my opinion it is no use making the law easy to understand or the layman will go away thinking he understands everything when in fact he's deluded. I've written a poem about it would you like to hear it? It's only twelve stanzas.

'An Englishman's home is his property;
And trespass is a crime like any othery,
A villain if caught – '

**Laura**  – Shurrup will yer! So you can't shoot no-one then?

**Lewis**  I didn't say that. It's all about what is *reasonable in the circumstances.*

*Sound of a car. Lights. LEWIS peaks through the curtains.*

It's Agar. If you plan to threaten to kill in self-defence I have a rather witty saying which I composed many years ago, which goes like this: 'If you mess with me, I'll get prosecuted, and you'll get buried.' You see if two parties are going to both raise the defence of self-defence it is generally speaking, *generally speaking*, better to be the living one. The deceased, *in my experience*, is rarely in a position to need to plead self-defence.

*Knock at the door. LEWIS opens it, after nodded permission from LAURA. Enter the young squire. YOUNG AGAR is aged 30-ish and dressed in quality tweeds.*

Good evening.

**Young Agar**  Okay.

*Silence.*

**Laura**  (*To AGAR.*) D'yer want the house then?

**Young Agar**  No.

**Laura**  It's a good house. Been good to me. You get Uncle Will's barn chucked in.

**Young Agar**  I expect Mr Lewis will advise you correctly to wait for someone from town with more money than sense for a sale of the house.

**Laura**  I don't trust him though. He's mad. Aren't yer? I said yer mad.

**Lewis**  I prefer 'eccentric'.

**Laura**  So you just want the sheds? They're good Warcup sheds.

**Young Agar**  We have been over this so many times Mrs Harrison. Yes. I just want the sheds.

**Laura**  I coulda bin your mother! I'm not signing. Not tonight.

**Young Agar**  (*Big sigh of frustration.*) I'm going. Mr Lewis. In future, I'm not coming out. You can phone me, but I'm not coming out to negotiate. You're wasting my time Mrs Harrison, and I have to say there feels as if there's something deliberate about it. Why will you not sign tonight? What's tonight's reason?

**Laura**  It's the lottery tonight. I might win. I been feeling lucky all day.

**Young Agar**  Goodnight.

**Laura**  I'll sign tomorrow if I don't win.

*YOUNG AGAR leaves. LAURA fiddles with the TV. She finds the Saturday night lottery show.*

I onny wanna listen to the draw. Can't stand all that smarm.

*LAURA turns the TV down.*

**Lewis**  What would you do if you won the lottery?

**Laura**  I'd get that washing machine fixed.

**Lewis**  You could start again. With the pigs.

**Laura**  An't got no labour.

**Lewis**  Yes, not having Titch with us any longer makes all the difference.

*LEWIS looks at the beam with something approaching distaste. On the hook is a small posy of flowers.*

What about those two young Polish men?

**Laura**  They was good workers but they upped and offed to Birmingham.

**Lewis**  I've always wanted to know from what or from whom they were seeking refuge.

**Laura**  They were gay. Conscripted wan't they, and gerrin bullied an'all. So they said.

**Lewis**  Gay pigmen? I suppose it could happen.

*A bit of Dale Winton on the lottery show.*

**Laura**  Dale Winton. Is he gay?

**Lewis**  For his sake, I hope so. I love to watch a man who's found his niche.

Tomorrow! Mañana! À demain!

**Laura**  Aye.

**Lewis**  Lock this door!

*Exit Mr LEWIS. LAURA prepares for herself a bowl of cornflakes with sugar on top. She sits and eats them. The door opens slowly and BLUE peeks out. BLUE walks up to behind LAURA and then steps in front of her.*

**Blue**  Shhh!

*LAURA stands, uttering nothing but a whine.*

Sit down love. We're not gonna hurt you. If you do what we say, you won't get hurt. We both got mothers we love.

**Danny**  Alright? Finish your cornflakes.

**Blue**  We want the gun, and then we'll be off, alright?

**Danny**  We can't find the key. Where's the fucking key!?

**Blue**  Shut it you fucking daft chav. Chill alright. Sorry mum. Now then, where's the key?

*LAURA has the key round her neck on a chain. She lifts the chain over her head.*

Lovely. Sweet.

*BLUE goes over to the cabinet and opens it. There are no guns in it.*

Where's the gun, mum?

**Danny**   Where's the fucking gun?!

*LAURA whines a bit more and then DANNY smacks her in the mouth with his fist.*

You want some, eh!?

*BLUE drags DANNY off her.*

**Blue**   What you fucking doing? Don't be a cunt! Respect! Alright!?

(*To LAURA.*) I'm sorry love. He's well out of order.

(*To DANNY.*) Get over there.

**Danny**   It was only a little smack Blue.

*BLUE walks over to DANNY and takes him downstage.*

**Blue**   (*Whispering.*) What's my name?

**Danny**   (*Whispering.*) Fuck. Did I? Sorry.

(*Loud.*) Sorry Paddy.

**Blue**   Once we got the gun we're off. By law you gotta keep it in the case. Where is it love? I'm not gonna hurt you love, but just tell me where the gun is. I'm a decent bloke. I respect you.

**Danny**   I'll give her a slap.

*BLUE holds off DANNY.*

**Blue**   Do you see?

*LAURA whines. DANNY picks a knife from the kitchen top and thrusts his hand under LAURA's clothes to her crotch threatening her with the knife.*

**Danny**  Open yer legs or I'll rip yer head off and shit down yer neck! I bet you fucking stink down there.

**Blue**  Oh bloody hell.

**Danny**  Lovely!

*DANNY pushes LAURA onto the floor on her back, and straddles her, all the time feeling under her skirt. The lights and TV go to black suddenly.*

What the fuck's going on?

**Blue**  You on a meter?

**Laura**  No.

**Danny**  Where's the fuse-box?

**Laura**  In t'lobby.

**Blue**  Shh! I can fucking hear someone. Shh!

*DANNY goes over to the door in the back wall and opens it, knife in hand. WILLIAM is in the doorway sitting in a motorised wheelchair, dressed in pyjamas, in the dark. He is now 109, with long white hair. He rests a shotgun in his lap. He has one hand on a length of string which goes to the fuse-box above his head. He pulls the string and the lights flash on. There is a moment of tableau. Then WILLIAM shoots DANNY at very close range, and DANNY collapses dead.*

No mate, no mate, no. Please. No mate, please mate no. I an't hurt no-one. She's alright. Please mate. We're just doing a bit of nicking. She an't been touched, mate, honest, I an't touched her. Please mate, please.

**William**  Don't call me 'mate'. It's annoying.

**Blue**  I been decent with the woman, ask her please.

**Laura**  I'm alright dad.

**William**  (*To LAURA.*) Who was that in the cars?

**Laura**  Mr Lewis and the young squire.

**William**  What's that nutter Lewis want now?

**Laura**  Dad! You know very well what we're doing.

**William**  Who's gerrin the sheds?

**Laura**  I told yer. The squire'll buy the sheds. Best to try and gerr a townie to buy the house.

**William**  Worr about my barn?

**Laura**  House and barn. Sheds separate.

**William**  Did we win lottery?

**Laura**  They an't had it yet. I've felt lucky all day.

**William**  Empty your pockets. Mate.

*BLUE complies, taking out the wedding ring, and the war medals.*

**Blue**  Military medal. That'll be yours yeah?

**William**  Aye.

**Blue**  I respect you. I honour you. You lost your legs in the war as well, I guess. I respect that. How did you lose your legs?

**William**  Tank ran over them.

**Blue**  Filthy fucking Germans eh.

**William**  The Germans din't have tanks.

**Blue**  We don't do enough history nowadays do we?

You didn't die though, eh.

**William**  There's an angel for farmers. Obviously not one for burglars. Where's me letter from the Queen?

**Blue**  I an't touched your letter mister.

**William**  It's still in the safe then?

**Blue**  Yeah.

**William**  Open the safe up love.

*LAURA takes a screwdriver from the drawer and opens the safe.*

**Blue**  You're not gonna like this. So before you get upset let me tell you that it was Danny, him, who did this, in the safe. It was him.

*LAURA brings the safe over, looking at the contents as she does.*

He was a nutter.

*WILLIAM has a look in the safe.*

**William**  Where's my letter?

**Blue**  It's underneath. It wan't really about you. He never liked the Queen. His sister's half Irish.

**William**  Go pick that kitchen knife up off the top there.

*BLUE picks up the knife.*

**Blue**  Please. Don't shoot. I'll do anything.

**William**  I don't want you to do owt.

**Blue**  Don't kill me please. I'll do anything.

**William**  Hold it t'other way round. Like yer stabbing.

**Blue**  No, please. Don't shoot.

*BLUE turns the knife around.*

**William**  Kneel down. Shuffle towards me. That's enough.

**Blue**  Please don't shoot. I'll do anything.

**William**  You comfortable?

**Blue**  Yeah. Thank you.

**William**  Get comfortable. We're gonna watch the lottery.

*The lottery draw is done, in silence. They get one number somewhere in the middle of the draw. This is seen by a glance between LAURA and WILLIAM. LAURA doesn't need to check her numbers, she knows them off by heart, but she does hold her ticket. She turns the TV off.*

You ever worked for a living?

**Blue**  What?

**William**  We got good sheds, but we an't got no labour.

**Laura**  We need a pigman.

**Blue**  Yeah. Alright. What do you want me to do?

**William**  Raise pigs.

**Blue**  Yes. I'll do that. Please, please don't shoot. I like pigs.

**Willliam**  Have you ever used a steam pressure washer?

**Blue**  I could learn.

**William**  It's all hard work, pigs, but it's fun.

**Laura**  If one of them gets out. That's funny, in't it dad. That's always funny.

**William**  Aye. Yer'll stink of pigs.

**Blue**  I don't mind.

**William**  Yer shower, yer bath, two, three times a day. Yer can't get rid of it. Yer happy to shower twice a day and live with the nagging disappointment that everyone thinks yer need a bath?

**Blue**  That wouldn't be a problem.

**William**  Yer car stinks of pigs, yer wife stinks of pigs.

**Blue**  Okay. That's cool.

**Laura**  Yer can get used to owt if yer have to.

**William**  Yer DVD player'll stink of pigs.

**Laura**  Yer DVDs'll stink of pigs.

**William**  Yer DVD disk cleaning kit'll stink of pigs. Yer could live like that and still keep a song in yer heart could yer, cos if yer couldn't do it with a song in yer heart I'll shoot yer dead now.

**Blue**  I'd sing all day. I can do it.

**William**  Could you collect from a boar? Yer catch the sperm in a flask, and if you have to yer give it an helping hand. Yer could check yer sows, see if they're 'ot could yer? You could press their backs, see if she's ready…

**Blue**  Yup. Don't shoot please.

**William**  Could yer open yer post in a morning?

**Blue**  Yeah.

**William**  From the bank?

**Blue**  Yes.

**William**  From the feed company?

**Blue**  Yeah. Please don't shoot.

**William**  Yer could read yer post from the ministry eh?

**Blue**  Yes.

**William**  Yer could open yer bills from the vet could yer, and still be fun to live with?

**Blue**  Yeah.

**Laura**  Yer could open yer post from Brussels, could yer? You could open it, read it, read it again, and read it a third time, and still not understand it, and go and see your solicitor, and pay him to read it and explain it yer, and still not understand it and worry all day about whether you're stupid, and believe the whole world has gone mad, and you're the only sane person left, and read it again, and not believe it again. And the next day open a letter from your bank, and another from the feed company, and the bill from your solicitor and put your gear on and –

**William**  – with a song in yer heart!

**Laura**  – go round yer sheds and care for yer pigs, look at them every day, follow their health.

**William**  Look at each and every one, and really care, not cos yer love the pig itself, but because if yer don't yer not doing yer job cos if yer don't look at every pig every day then one day one of them'll have P double R S or swine fever and yer'd be wiped out over night.

**Laura**  That's not worr happened to us!

**William**  And yer wife'll have to go and work in the Little Chef. Yer could do that could yer?

**Laura**  And keep singing.

**Blue**  I imagine, it's a hard life, is it?

**Laura**  It's enough to mek a monkey bite its young.

**William**  And you wunt let that worry get to yer, and you could make love to your wife?

**Laura**  Could yer make love to yer wife?

**Blue**  Yeah.

**William**  You could adore her; worship her; and make her feel beautiful and blessed and glad she married a pig farmer and not James Bond. Yer could do that could yer?

*BLUE breaks down and cries. He's beyond it.*

**Blue**   Yes! I'll do it. I'll give it a go. Don't shoot please.

**William**   I think we just gorr ourselves a new pigman.

*To black.*

**THE END**

# Research Interviews

## Simon Cherry

Richard Bean interviews the vet Simon Cherry BVM&S; MRCVS.

**RB** Why did they all go out of business?

**SC** The pig farmers who had the worst time were the farmers who borrowed money to set up reasonably expensive buildings only to find that the market was cut underneath them by cheaper imports from Holland.

**RB** Why is Dutch pig meat cheaper?

**SC** We went about improving welfare of pigs before the Europeans did.

**RB** Why?

**SC** Politicians. We were in the EC... the animal welfare legislation there is a European-wide one and the national governments can do whatever gold-plating on top of that. And animal welfare is something that we as a nation are exercised about, and the politicians decided that factory farming had been moving too far away from the rights of the animal. Our vets go into the docks every week and there's pig meat coming in from Holland the equivalent of sixty to eighty thousand pigs a week coming in through the docks. It's backs to produce bacon. And we can't compete now.

**RB** What aspects of inhumane, if that's the word, inhumane treatment did we ban before the Europeans?

**SC** Stalls and tethering essentially. Sows were tied up for weeks on end and that was frowned on, it was a sort of collar, attached to a link chain which was attached to the floor, and the advantage is that they were easier to manage, and you could get more pigs per building. You could see what each individual sow was doing, you could feed it individually, you could care for it individually, easier for health examining, and you could get more sows per building.

**RB** But we banned those methods before our competitors in Europe, I mean, countries supposedly in the same trading union as us?

**SC** Quite. I think it had run its day. I was on the committee which rebuilt the Bishop Burton college unit and this was back in the eighties and we looked at the way farming was going, about banning stalls and tethers, and we thought this sort of thing is getting phased out, and it came rather quicker than we expected and we went down to look at the MAFF experimental farms who were experimenting in animal management techniques and they'd got the idea of these computer-controlled transponders from the dairy industry. It's a collar and it triggers a computer which feeds it the right amount of food. They could be fed very accurately, and we adapted them for pigs, you could loose house pigs, then you had feeding stations and you trained them to go for the food, you had to train a new generation of gilts. We thought this was the way things were going to go. The whole loose house system is a big success. They tend to gather in little groups. It's always the same group of sows. Which teats they suckle on. Hierarchy. Even the runts form a hierarchy.

**RB** But the Europeans still tether them in stalls?

**SC** At the time you're talking about yes. There was something like a ten year window to apply the legislation.

**RB** That's nuts.

**SC** A lot of well run pig farms went out of business.

**RB** What I mean is, everyone in the EC should be following the same rules at the same time.

**SC**  Huh! The Europeans are having to catch up with that legislation now. All the farmers used to argue that Brussels made the rules out of some entirely misguided conception, we, the UK that is, gold-plated them, and applied them straight away and every other European country just ignored them.

**RB**  So what now, British farmers have to find niche markets for their more expensive pork?

**SC**  You can't feed the nation on organic. You just have to literally walk down any supermarket's aisles and you'll see hundreds of thousands of packs of bacon, and none of it's organic. The majority of the British population buy on price. We as vets say to the supermarkets, 'Why don't you encourage more welfare?' They say, 'Organic is such a small part of our turnover. It doesn't sell, and we have to downgrade it, and reprice it before it goes out of date.'

**RB**  What, so if I buy cheap bacon it might have been organic bacon that no-one was willing to pay the price for, and then got relabelled? ·

**SC**  That's what they tell us they do. There's a section of the market which will only buy on price. There's another section where quality is important but they look at the price, then there's a big section where people look at value, which is a complex concept. There's a big chunk, the biggest chunk, where they just shop on price. The one section to be squeezed will be the value section.

**RB**  I've been interviewing pig farmers, or ex-pig farmers, and I was surprised... You see I always ask the same questions – what was the funniest thing that ever happened, and what was the worst thing about being a pig farmer – and I was surprised when they said that having to kill an animal really upset them.

**SC**  Oh yes. Most of the pig farmers put animals down on the farm in an emergency. You do it for a reason. Most farmers are extremely conscious of welfare. We've been and done operations on farms and caesarians on old cows and things which must be totally uneconomic for the farmer, but they say, 'I've had this cow for sixteen years she doesn't owe me anything, and I'm not gonna shoot her just cos she can't calve herself at this age.' They don't see animals as so many pound signs. The happier their pigs are the better from their point of view.

**RB** Who owns the pigs on the farms that survive?

**SC** Mostly the feed company puts the pigs into a unit. The feed company will put the pigs into a farm and the farmer will supply the labour and the building and the feed company will supply everything else. The arable farmers have sometimes got together to start a feed company, it's their grain that makes the feed, after all. They'll supply the grain that makes the feed. And they'll take the pigs away at the end. For example, they might have a contract to supply an abattoir, who in turn are in a scheme with a supermarket.

**RB** Where's the power?

**SC** Supermarkets. They will always look after their bottom line. And it's the primary producer who will get squeezed. Tesco's say, 'Why don't you all get together and bargain with us?', but they know that farmers will never do that. But Europe has led to all sorts of problems. The French and German farming lobbies were more powerful than ours. We've done well out of the EU because our efficient farmers, the arable farmers, get a great deal of money in grants, grants they don't need actually, but not the pig and poultry farmers. The arable and cereal farmers get grants they don't need, and the pig and poultry men have never got a penny. They were all selling finished pigs at a loss in the end. It was a farce.

**RB** What about Foot and Mouth?

**SC**   From the disease point of view it would have completely decimated the pig industry round here but we were lucky, in the East Riding we were unaffected.

**RB**   So our farmers were wiped out by a combination of British sentimentality about animals, Europe, and the supermarkets – is that what you are saying?

**SC**   Well, we didn't get Foot and Mouth put it that way.

# John Hart and Gwen Hart

John Hart and Gwen Hart (pig farmers in the East Riding
of Yorkshire from the 1950s to the 1990s) talk to Richard
Bean.

**JH**  My grandad had the farm about three miles from here. I
was born in Preston, then we moved out to Burstwick, but
I'd been on a pig farm all me life working with me dad
since nine. It was a general farm but he had pigs had on it.
Aye, me dad had been running pigs there from the mid-
forties. They were all in sties in them days. They weren't
all outdoors ten or twenty in a pen all fed with a bucket.
Maybe, two hundred and fifty pigs, fattening pigs, didn't
have any sows. He just bought them in and fattened them
up. Breeding down on the farm. Sort of arcs with an outside
run to them. I was always with me dad. He'd give us a
croggy down there. It was weekends. Thorne school, and
walk back to Burstwick, I got the job of taking lunches at
harvest time, and I'd take the basket to the Irish lads, just
at harvest time, they used to live in the granary, sleep on
bags of chaff.

Me granny would supply us all with food and tea. We used
horses. But to do the land work, the real heavy work we
had a Ford, open top radiator, you could see the water in it.
One of the old pop pop ones. You started them with a firing
cartridge, and you had to hit them with an hammer. Great
big bang, to start the tractor, pop pop. I used to ride horses
and that, when we used to lead corn in, pull them on from
stook to stook. Then we moved up from Fords to the old
Nuffields. I remember going off in a morning and putting
bags round us waist cos chaffs would be damp so you
wouldn't get wet cos stooks would be wet. You'd put them
round yer legs so you wouldn't get wet. Just a hessian sack.

**RB**  What's a chaff?

**JH**   A chaff is…hard to explain. A stook is made up of eight or ten chaffs. Pieces of corn and straw, just tied in the middle, all done in them days with an old binder. And it's just tied in the middle, cos they used to be done then with an old binder. You used to go along behind them. Load it onto trailers and stack it in the stack yard. This time of year and they'd come round with their threshing sets, a threshing gang would come. It was Burhams from Burstwick. It used to go into a big bailer which tied them up with wire. As kids it was our job to chase the mice, cats and dogs.

**RB**   I heard your mother moved to a farm without ever seeing it!?

**JH**   Aye, we went to Aldbrough. I was nine years old. He set up his own farm. Only four acres. Four acre field. 1956. Me mum went there without actually having seen it, aye.

**GH**   I used to take his younger brother on walks when we was teenage sweethearts.

**JH**   Me dad borrowed a steam pressure washer. We went across one morning and pressure washed it all day. Me dad wanted it clean. We weren't even breeding. He went round all the local farmers and bought the little weeners. He'd go to market every Monday an Wednesday.

**RB**   What about feed?

**JH**   We used to mix it ourselves in the shed. Me uncle used to grind it for us into bags. He used to bring the meal through to us. Mix it with water and mek up your ration with a bit of water. Most nights when we'd come home from school we'd work on the farm. We had twenty pens, ten down either side. 200 odd pigs. The slurry we'd barrow and shovel, and shovel it out the end. It was all solid muck and straw. It all went into a big heap. We had a deal with a local farmer. We used to get his straw, and he used to get our muck. Exchange. It was hard work. It's always hard work. But to me, it was a fun. Used to work right through the summer. We had poultry.

We had hundreds of eggs. Me mam used to stand at the sink washing them.

**RB**  Who bought your finished pigs?

**JH**  They were all sold to a bacon factory, slaughterhouse. Yorkshire Farmers bacon factory. Sometime in the week the number would be organised. We always aimed at 200 pounds, for a finishing weight. Everything was castrated.

**RB**  How did you find time to play for Hull City?

**JH**  (*Laughs.*) Our Brian was working at home. I went footballing, then came back into the business when I was twenty-one. Eventually we got up to 1200 pigs. We bought a farm at Cowden. It was me dad at first, the partnership. In a short period of time we bought two more farms. It was a general farm with no real accommodation for pigs.

**GH**  My dad was a butcher. If you had odd batches of pigs in and they used to fight and we often had to call the butcher out to slaughter one. This can be six in the morning of course. What pigs tend to do is they go round and round and set about the weakest pig and set about it, and it's absolutely jiggered. It's either gonna die or you slaughter it. The butcher would come round with his knife, and if the meat was any good, you'd have some of it. He'd cut it's throat and bleed it. I used to go and watch me dad slaughter. When I was a kid I'd be there eating me sweets and watching him cut their throats and drain the blood. Me granny never could understand it cos I used to go out, you know, I'd belt round the butcher at half past five, and we'd get this one dragged out, and we'd cut its throat and hang it up and bleed it and there's blood all over, and a right mess, and then I'd eat this great big breakfast and me gran could never understand how we could eat it. You never thought anything of it, well I didn't any road.

**JH**  At that time our Brian had been running sows of his own. Fifty sows. Started before he left school. There was a deep litter chicken house. We converted the place to tethers. Put a collar round its neck and the pig can move backwards and forwards but that's all. We led them up one day and what a going-on, I think me dad's arms were about six foot long by the end of the day. You had to get in behind them while someone put the collars on. Some of these were great big old sows you know 300, 400, 500 lbs. Tethering lasted but not long for us. Until it became illegal. Early nineties. I think they give ten years until it was illegal. Six months time it'll be illegal.

**RB**  What are the advantages of tethering?

**JH**  Tethers, you confine the sow with short rails between them, tied with a neck tie, whereas with stalls it's like a crate, you put bars behind them, they're loose in as much as they aren't tied with a neck but still confined. Farrowing crate is a different area altogether. The thing about stalls is that they are still free. You can take the backs off them stalls and they won't go nowhere.

**RB**  What breed of pig were you running?

**JH**  Large White or Large White Landrace Cross. The only time we took pure Landrace in was when we wanted to breed with them. To get the crosses we needed. We started with fifty sows and when we finished we had 300. Finishers. We ended up with three or four thousand pigs. We were selling weaners to a bloke from south.

**RB**  Are these pigs in sheds?

**JH**  Loose housed in groups. Groups of three sows. Dry sows. When you've just taken them off from weaning, or when they're in pig, you know, when they're ready to fire again. They were like stalls, there was a pen with three separate divisions in it, and there was drinkers there. They was loose housed on straw.

**RB**  What's a typical working day like?

**JH**   Feeding for a start, we would be, when we were right up to 300 sows it used to tek us from 7:30 to 10:00 to get all the feeding done. Even though it was automatic.

**RB**   Everyone tells me that running pigs is all about converting feed into meat.

**JH**   Of course. Originally we used to mix up our feed ourselves then we bought it in from a compounder, a feed company, we'd done various things, our own formulation, we bought in a compromise. The vets helped us, they visited about every three months. In the early days it was either with a scoop or a bucket. We always fed the sows with litters individually, well because there's so many changes in what they need. When they first farrow maybe you cut them down to a pound a day or something, or two pound a day. By the time they've finished mebbe you're giving them as much as they can eat. There was three of us, four?

**GH**   Our middle daughter did all the farrowing side for ten years. They all enjoyed it, school leavers. They could get stuck into it. If they come with us they had a shovel in their hand or a scoop or whatever. Carl (*Laughs.*) out of Hull, he didn't even know what a pig was.

**JH**   We sold everything off the farm for bacon. We were selling them through part of a marketing group called Feedex, Newpork, it was a marketing group started by all the vets. It was sold on actually, through Scotlean, a Scottish based thing.

**RB**   How did that work on a week-by-week basis?

**GH**   Beginning of the week we'd let them know how many pigs we thought we had.

**JH**   We used to weigh them and mark those that was ready to go. Then they'd come on a Friday morning and load them up, and they'd go away to the slaughterhouse, to Malton bacon factory, down to Spalding, I mean at one stage Malton were slaughtering 40,000 pigs a week. 1997. I don't think they exist as a slaughterhouse any more.

**RB** Did the business grow steadily, or what?

**JH** In the sixties I was still playing for Hull City. I packed up the football as a job in about 1968.

**GH** I was working for the solicitors. When I moved up to Hill Top I was pregnant with Nicola. We were getting the first sheds ready and we were hopeful, really.

**JH** Pigs were fairly profitable at that time. I can remember me dad talking money to us, he was getting twenty pound for a 200 lb bacon pig. And making a profit on that. That's a six-month old pig, well in those days a little bit older.

**GH** We'd got married we was starting a family. We was building the unit up, we were starting from scratch. We were borrowing money from the bank, they were very positive about that, no problem. The bank was still lending us money.

**JH** I'd borrowed £18,000 from the bank to do some work to cover the new legislation, and that was only a year before we went bust. Within the four months we'd lost most of it. We weren't selling at the right price.

**GH** In the seventies we were doing quite well. In a sense rosy. The pig industry was a good industry. We were mixing our own feed, or later on we became part of a group called Grinder Mix, it was a mobile milling machine – he used to come round the farms and we bought the raw materials and he used to come round the farms and mix it, mill it and mix it, for us and blow it into the bins for us, we used to buy all our materials, cereals and that from the local farmers.

**JH** Aye, the seventies was quite lucrative years. In fact in '76 we actually bought some land.

**RB** Did you borrow money to buy the land?

**JH**    Yes. We bought the land partly to produce some feed of our own, and partly because of the problems of muck and slurry, and partly cos we needed straw. We bought seventy odd acres and then we ended up with nearly a hundred acres. It was nothing like enough, it seemed like a lot of money to shell out the time.

**GH**    It was actually for Brian at Cowden, wasn't it.

**JH**    His farm at Cowden…he was having to buy straw, the cereals we could always use that, and it give us more options with muck and slurry. If you've got 300 sows you get a lot of muck and slurry. The amount of land we had wasn't nearly enough to put all our slurry on, but we could get rid of the rest cos they all wanted it, chalky land – it could be a problem with your slurry, with your water courses. For us up at where we were we always had an arrangement with Geoff Kayley and they had 800 acres at Aldbrough and we had a written agreement with them that they would provide us with straw and we'd put muck and slurry on their land. They would bale straw for us if we wanted but we normally did it ourselves, and led it off ourselves. He was really happy with it cos he was getting lots of muck on his land. We did all the work on it ourselves apart from ploughing. Me dad's base was general farming and he knew it all. I always have been interested in machinery. So we did that ourselves, extra to doing the pigs. Leading straw, 26,000 bales per year for the three units. It was all handled mechanically.

**RB**    What did you grow?

**JH**    Wheat and barley. We used rape as a break. Instead of growing peas or potatoes.

**RB**    What was different in the eighties?

**JH**    It was just an ongoing development.

**GH**    End of seventies we had 200 sows and were doing quite well, I guess.

**JH**  We never spent really freely. I can remember after getting into the partnership going to me dad to borrow money to go on holiday. We weren't struggling. We had holidays. Through the eighties into the nineties there was always blip years. We never felt we were pushed financially. Two bad years out of three. Usually disease.

**RB**  What diseases?

**GH**  TGE. Transmissable Gastro Enteritis. TGE. There's always been the things coming in like your TGEs.

**JH**  Right through my experience there was always the risk of disease. Birds can carry it.

**RB**  What did you worry about at night?

**JH**  Nothing. You were knackered! You went straight to sleep.

**GH**  Money.

**JH**  Aye, well. I would often go to bed at night, and the last thing I'd done is go round the pigs. Sometimes it was two o'clock at night before I got to bed, and other times I was up all night if they was farrowing, mebbe I'd had two hours sleep. Sometimes I'd be up by half five.

**GH**  Buildings. We was always thinking of new buildings.

**JH**  Aye, we'd go to the bank say look this is what we're planning, these are the figures, performance-wise, it all comes down to how many pigs per sow per year and what your costs are. Some of it unfortunately was to do with legislation. You had to spend thousands of pounds to stand still, and in some case go backwards. You couldn't keep as many pigs in the same space as before.

**GH**  There was a lot of argy bargy in the eighties about tethers and stalls.

**RB**  How would you know about legislation?

**JH**    Every year there was a pig fair down at Stoneleigh, Coventry. We used to go down there. The ministry was there, the manufacturers, feeding systems, breeding companies. May.

**GH**    And Government inspectors. Ministry of AG. Generally forewarned. Just safety officers coming on. To belong to the scheme you used to have to have a ministry inspection and get yourself stamped. You had to have a vet on every three months. It was run by the government. At one stage you couldn't sell your pigs to the slaughterhouse unless you were stamped. You had to pay to be on it, a lot of the stuff they were saying was absolutely stupid, like the number of drinkers you had to have to a pen, how many pigs you could have in a certain amount of space, straw, how much straw, what you could and couldn't do. By then we'd stopped castrating anyhow, everything had to be tattooed so they could trace them through the slaughterhouse.

**JH**    In the nineties it was impossible. The financial pressures were from the government with legislation, supermarkets buying cheap meat from abroad. We were losing thousands of pounds a week. The prices just collapsed. There was too much pig meat about. Holland was the problem. I think some of it was coming from further away but we'll never know, the story was that some of it was coming into Holland from countries we weren't supposed to take it from, processed in Holland and then passed on to us as Dutch meat. We could never prove that. As a nation we'd developed quite rapidly and we were overproducing pig meat.

**GH**    The French carried on with stalls which they weren't supposed to do and they subsidised their farmers to set up new units, and at one stage they were taking cereal or barley out of stock, out of store in this country, and selling it to Spain for £30 a ton when in this country we were paying £70 or £80 a ton. No-one was interested, I mean, no-one's interested in farming in this country are they, and we asked the government to sell the stockpiles to us cheap and they wouldn't, but they sold it to the French. In Europe they were developing systems which were theoretically illegal in this country.

**JH** Feed prices were quite expensive. The feed companies they kept it as tight as they could, they were very supportive in lots of ways, they allowed us lots of credit. We always used to pay at the end of the month following, and then it got to be three months credit, thirty days from the end of the month, it's very tying in when you get into that situation, you're stuck with them, which is what they want of course.

**GH** We were still selling to Newpork. The price got down to something like 70p for a kilogram when we'd been getting £1.20 a kilogram at the top. You're selling a seventy kilo pig. We would have needed to be selling at £1.10 or £1.20 for a ninety kilo pig. Imagine if what you need to make a small profit, a small margin, is £1.10. Imagine then what a loss you're making at 70p.

**RB** Where's the power in the market?

**JH** The supermarket. You can never pin a supermarket down, they said to us that we had to be a member of this pig scheme before and adhering to the rules of this scheme, then they would buy our pigs, and then put British on it, but if it was bought from abroad and then processed in this country they only had to slice it and it was called British meat.

**GH** We was out picketing, we went in bus-loads to the big depots, Asda and Tesco's, we had a big meeting in Blackpool and then met the ministry. The ministry would say anything to appease you and then ignore it.

**RB** The British public's perception of the farmer is someone in a Barbour jacket, driving a Range Rover, and a regular fat cheque from Brussels.

**JH**   Never had a penny.

**RB**   Come on!?

**GH**   Nothing.

**JH**   We was a primary pork unit. Pork and poultry. That's outside the grant thing. Not during my time. Never got a penny. The arable men, who generally don't need it, they got it all. One of them I know has almost said he doesn't want it. Cos it wasn't doing farming any good.

**RB**   How, or when did you decide to pack it in?

**GH**   We'd been umming and ahhing for a long time.

**JH**   We'd had two bad years out of three. And we said we got to call it a day. Me dad died. I'm glad me dad never saw the farms go, so that was a good thing.

**GH**   Whatever we did we couldn't make anything like enough money to keep going. The bank knew what was happening and they were very good. They talked it through with us. He sat down. He said you're gonna get some letters, and they're gonna be unpleasant letters but as long as you've not been trying to fiddle us you'll be alright, we'll be straight with you, but if you have, we'll come down on you like a ton of bricks. The bank manager suggested I go into business consultancy. I think what with the supermarkets running things the margins we'd been used to would never come back.

**RB**   How much did you owe the bank?

**JH**   £200,000. Plus our houses. They took the houses and the farm.

**GH**   If you've done forty years you think you've earned summat.

**JH**   You satisfied everybody. You satisfied the ministry, you satisfied the vet, you satisfied the bloody slaughterhouses with the right pigs, you satisfied breeding companies, and you ended up with absolutely nowt for yersen.

**GH** You was just working for nothing, seven days a week, and doing it all for nowt.

**JH** I do this clerical job at the yard now, this job I've got now, and I think to mesen I don't know why I ever bothered working that hard. But there's not the same job satisfaction.

**GH** We envisaged not working at our age. I'm not saying we were expecting to be living in Barbados, but I don't think we thought we'd still be working at our age.

**RB** Okay it was hard work, but you enjoyed it?

**JH** I liked the countryside. I enjoyed doing that. We had a lot of fun. If one of them got out that was always funny! (*Laughs.*)

**GH** (*Laughs.*) We had a big boar got out. Mebbe 500 pounds.

**JH** And them pigs got into the slurry pit, some of them had got through the outside cover. (*Laughs.*)

**RB** What do you think of politicians?

**JH** It's just the way it is I'm afraid in that sort of position. They don't care between elections. The words come out, but they don't mean what they say. I wouldn't trust a politician as far as I could chuck them.

# Other plays by Richard Bean
## published by Oberon Books

| | |
|---:|:---|
| *Toast* | (ISBN 184002 104 7) |
| *Under the Whaleback* | (ISBN 184002 286 8) |
| *Honeymoon Suite* | (ISBN 184002 406 2) |
| *The Mentalists* | (ISBN 184002 287 6) |
| *The God Botherers* | (ISBN 184002 415 1) |
| *Smack Family Robinson* | (ISBN 184002 373 2) |
| *Mr England* | (ISBN 184002 170 5) |

*The Mentalists*, *Under the Whaleback* and *The God Botherers* are now also available in a volume:

*Richard Bean Plays One*   (ISBN 184002 569 7)